Emory Adams Allen

Scenes Abroad

Emory Adams Allen

Scenes Abroad

ISBN/EAN: 9783337419851

Printed in Europe, USA, Canada, Australia, Japan

Cover: Foto ©Thomas Meinert / pixelio.de

More available books at **www.hansebooks.com**

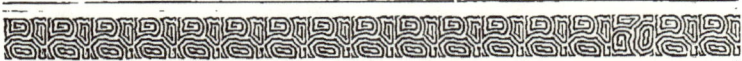

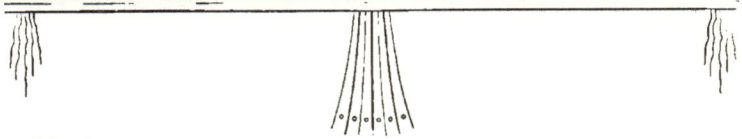

SCENES ABROAD

OR

Gems of Travel for the Home Circle

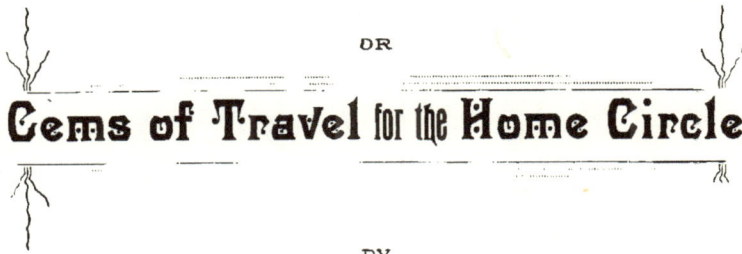

BY

E. A. ALLEN

AUTHOR OF "GOLDEN GEMS OF LIFE," "BIBLE COMPANION" ETC.

CINCINNATI—NASHVILLE—ATLANTA:
CENTRAL PUBLISHING HOUSE.
1890.

❦ Preface. ❦

T the present day it is not necessary to speak of the value of books giving us information as to the world at large. Modern civilization, with its daily papers, its railroads, and telegraphs, has virtually annihilated distance, and we are expected to be familiar with the history of foreign lands, to know their peculiarities, and to be acquainted with the various interesting scenes to be witnessed in their midst.

Many books have been written to supply this information. Celebrated travelers have written most entertainingly of what they have themselves observed, and guide books and encyclopedias abound. It is evident, then, that we can not flatter ourselves that we have in our possession a mass of facts not previously known. We can, however, put forth some claims in regard to this book which we trust will be readily admitted, and will result in giving it a cordial welcome.

We have endeavored to give, in a very limited compass, a description accompanied by illustrations of the most celebrated scenes in the countries visited. We have interwoven with this description items of information concerning the history, customs, and peculiarities of the people themselves. In order to break the monotony of mere description, we have adopted the expedient of the story form of narrative, keeping before us a group of intelligent children, and supposed to be talking more particularly to them. We believe this will add greatly to the interest of the book. However, it is not solely a book for children, as a perusal of its pages will abundantly show. We trust it will be acceptable to all ages and classes, and believe it will be received by all as being in truth what its name implies, a description of Scenes Abroad.

CINCINNATI, OHIO, January 1, 1890.

E. A. Allen

TABLE OF CONTENTS.

(v)

✻ List of Illustrations. ✻

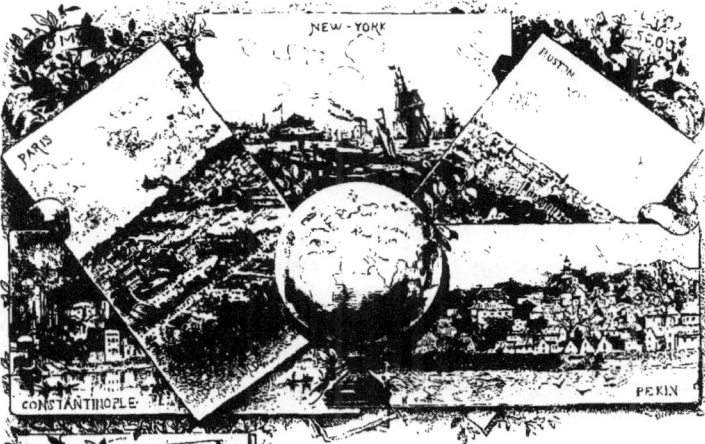

Scenes Abroad.

CHAPTER I.

INTRODUCTION.

I T was snowing!

Nothing remarkable about such an occurrence, to be sure; but just at this particular time and place it was received with marks of approval by all, unless we except the chronic grumblers and sundry unfortunate people who could scarcely keep warm even in bright and cheery weather. It was doubly welcome because the holiday season was at hand, and in our Eastern States Christmas without sleighing is but half Christmas. So the boys and girls and good people generally of Welton were quite resigned to their fate when the day opened with a brisk snow-storm. It had been threatening for several days, but Nature was taking her

time about it, and seemed anxious to impress on the weather-wise that they
did not know all her secrets yet. She had refused to make good the
"indications" of the daily papers, which for several days had read, "Snow,
followed by clearing, colder weather." The moon also had apparently lost
her power; for, though the crescent hung just right according to the "oldest
inhabitant" for stormy weather, nothing of the kind had followed. But
after tantalizing them all for some days, Nature had relented. During the
night the snow had steadily fallen, and the storm still continued.

The walks were but partially cleared; for what was the use of clearing
them off until the storm was over? Such at least was the conclusion of
numerous red-cheeked boys who were expected to clear off the walks in front
of their homes, though we are not sure but they had further in mind that
popular maxim among some boys of "Never do to-day what you can put off
until to-morrow." School time came, and in spite of the storm there were
but few absent; for, if you will only notice, the first good snow of the
season never keeps children in doors as subsequent ones do. Among the
scholars there were five who were eagerly looking forward to the night; and
as we are somewhat interested in this particular group, we may as well make
their acquaintance at once.

Two of these children were brothers, Willie and Burt Adams. Their
father lived on a farm right on the outskirts of town. There was but two
years difference in the ages of the boys; and though Burt was the younger
of the two, he was more of a scholar, and easily kept in the same grade as
his brother. The boys enjoyed the advantages of both country and town.
They had been brought up to work; they were strong and healthy, and in
many ways were envied by the town boys. Did they not have ponies to ride?
Did not all good things grow in their father's orchard? Were there not
great roomy barns, sheds, and stacks where they could play all sorts of
games? Thus could they count up the good things in the lives of Willie
and Burt—without, however, thinking it worth while to note the hard work
all this called for.

The other three children we are particularly interested in were Nettie,
Ida, and Henry Scott. Their father was a well-to-do merchant; their mother
was sister to Mr. Charles Adams, the father of Willie and Burt; so the children were cousins. Nettie and Ida, aged twelve and fourteen, were in the
same room at school as their cousins. Henry was the "baby," though he

vigorously objected to that title, since, as he was ten years old and had just
entered the grammar room, he was beginning to rank himself as one of the
big boys. In truth, he had just reached that blissful era of boyhood life in
which they have unlimited confidence in their own powers and possibilities—
a rosy dream which, in most cases, the next fifteen years effectually dissipates.

Now, what was it that kept running through the minds of these five
boys and girls during the day—that gave such a suppressed air of importance
to their movements—that led to such a mysterious conference between Henry
and the older boys at recess—that made the afternoon seem so very long and
sent them all hurrying home with a vague feeling of delight as soon as the
afternoon session closed? It is safe to say that all boys and girls will at once
understand their feelings when we tell them that only the night before word
had come from Aunt Mary, who lived with grandpa and grandma clear to the
other end of town, that a telegram had just been received from their Uncle
George that he had landed in New York, and was expected at the old homestead the day following; and Aunt Mary had further added that they had
better come up in the evening and bring the children, and thus welcome
Uncle George on his return.

The children had only seen Uncle George a few times. Years before,
during the oil excitement, he had drifted into Western Pennsylvania; and
after various ups and downs, a lucky venture had made his fortune in a few
days. He had but little relish for speculation, and had no desire to continue
in business. He had been a great reader and scholar, and now he found himself in position to gratify his long cherished plan of foreign travel. So,
investing his money, he had set out on a life of wandering. He had made
one or two trips home, but for short visits only. This time it was different.
His parents were now old; he had visited nearly every part of the world,
and at their urgent request was coming home to spend some time with them.

To say nothing of the delight of meeting Uncle George, the children
were glad enough to visit at grandpa's. The house was large and roomy,
right on the very edge of town. Years before, when they were young,
grandpa and grandma had moved "West," as it was then called—though we
wouldn't think of calling it "West" now—and engaged in farming. In time
came railroads; coal mines were opened, manufactories erected, and a prosperous town had grown up; and some of the old farm had been required for
building lots. They had, however, clung to the old homestead, but had fitted

it up with luxuries undreamed of in their younger days. Only one of the four children remained at home, but the others, with the exception of Uncle George, were in the immediate vicinity; and so we see that Grandpa and Grandma Adams had a good deal of sunshine in their old age; in fact, it seemed to fill the whole house, and so it is no wonder the young folks liked to visit them.

When the boys reached home, the storm had ceased. The days were now at their shortest, and a beautiful winter's night was already coming on. The sky was clearing off from the northwest; the moon, about half full, appeared to be hurrying on past the broken clouds as if anxious to reach the blue space beyond, and show what she could do to make the evening pleasant. The west was yet aglow, where the setting sun had broken out in a smiling adieu after a day given over to storms. A beautiful mantle of white covered all within sight, and the jingle of bells showed that sundry young people proposed to tend strictly to business while the sleighing lasted.

And how the boys did hurry! Chores were done with punctuality and dispatch. We trust the various animals composing the "stock" duly appreciated the haste and good-natured profusion with which their wants were supplied that particular evening. We are not sure but what the chickens, impressed with the preparatory bustle going on even before the boys came home from school, and feeling that events must move off "on time," went to roost a little earlier than usual. If there was any discontent, it must have been in the thoughts of the colts that John, the hired man, was currying. They may have viewed the evident preparations making for an evening out with distrust. They had seen the "bobbs" being put in readiness, hay flung into the box, robes and blankets arranged on the seats; and who knows what equine memories were awakened when the strings of bells were brought out and put in a convenient place? Still, to do them justice, we don't believe they objected, especially when they found that an extra feed was given them.

Then came supper—just such a supper as is provided in the home of a well-to-do and liberally minded farmer. Then the bundling up while John brought up the team. The colts were not only resigned to their fate, but, judging from the impatient tossing of heads, emphasized now and then by vigorous stamps of hoofs, were considering the advisability of trying the metal of their driver. If they could only get the start, what a nice wreck they could make of the sleigh to which they were hitched! But there was little opportunity for that. Farmer Adams had driven too many horses to give his frisky team any chances. So they settled down to a rapid trot, and all parties enjoyed the two miles drive to grandpa's.

In the meanwhile somewhat similar scenes had taken place at the house of Mrs. Scott, the married sister. Papa had come from business a full half hour earlier than usual; and when the children reached home, dinner was ready to be placed on the table. The coachman had got out the big double cutter; but as Mr. Scott was going along, and the drive was to be such a short one, his duties ended with getting everything in readiness. Not having so much to do, the Scott family were at grandpa's when Mr. Adams drove up.

Yes, Uncle George had come. No mistake about that. The good-natured bark of Watch, the big Newfoundland, seemed to say that he felt the weight of new responsibility. The fire in the grate glowed and snapped with strange energy as if it, too, wanted to make things cheery. The smile on grandpa's face was certainly brighter than usual. How glad they all were to see Uncle George! And how glad he was to see them! The children did feel just a little bashful; but we may be sure it did not last long. In less than five minutes Henry had informed Nettie that "Uncle George was just boss," and in just about the same length of time Burt had made an equally interesting discovery—those strange looking books on the center table contained nothing but pictures. Yes, pictures of foreign places, noted persons, and objects of interest; and though the titles were all down, there were many that he had never heard of before. And then the children busied themselves looking at the pictures; but one by one they tired of that, and were more interested in the story that Uncle George was telling about his voyage home—that is, all except Burt; he always was a queer boy. He liked to hear his uncle talk, but the pictures in the albums demanded fully half his attention. Every now and then he would find a picture of something that he had read all about: how that would interest him. He came to a fine view of the "Landing Stage of Liverpool," and just at that moment he heard his uncle telling a little incident of his going on board for his return trip at Liverpool. "Oh, uncle," he burst out, "did you go on board your steamer from here?" at the same time bringing him the book opened at the picture in question. "Why, sure enough," said his uncle; "I had forgotten I had that picture in my collection. Yes," he continued, "here is a picture of the principal landing at Liverpool. A little steam tender takes the passengers from here to the great ocean-going steamers."

Uncle George went on with his story, but Burt had suddenly thought of a great scheme. Why couldn't his uncle tell him all about those pictures? How many there were! How interesting it would all be! How much he could learn! If he only just felt a little better acquainted with his uncle— it might not be so interesting for him to go over them all; then, besides, it would take a great deal of time. These rather mixed thoughts were running through his mind when Aunt Mary left the room to arrange for refreshments.

Now Aunt Mary, according to the children's ideas, was more than an ordinary aunt. It was simply wonderful how she could arrange things. Her nephews and nieces had unlimited confidence in her ability to accomplish what she set about. It is not strange, therefore, that Burt almost unnoticed followed his aunt from the room.

Well, he saw his aunt, and explained the situation to her in a few words. Aunt Mary said she thought she could arrange it. And she did. She talked with the parents and with Uncle George, and talked to such good effect that after lunch, when the children were getting tired, Uncle George made a little speech. He told them that not only did he have the books shown on the center table, but he had many others in his room; and he had, besides, a great many interesting objects to talk about. He and Aunt Mary had been considering a plan to interest and instruct his nephews and nieces; and he was going to suggest that they meet every two weeks at grandpa's house, and he would talk to them about foreign lands.

"But now," he continued, "there is one condition. I shall take some pains to make my talk interesting, and your parents will see that you get here somehow. Aunt Mary will make it pleasant for you. But in order to get the most good out of the meetings, you must spend some time in reviewing your geography and history; and as we will meet in the library where the encyclopedia is handy, I shall probably have one of you read about some of the places we are supposed to visit, or the objects of interest we see, and expect you to take notes of what is said. This will require some little work on your part, but I am sure you will all agree to it."

And they did agree to it, though it must be added that Henry's assent was expressed by a gentle snore, as the little fellow had gone on a tour of his

own to the land of dreams.   But Uncle George observed, with a smile, that
they would not expect Henry to do a great deal of preparatory work, or to
make very extensive notes.   So it was arranged that on the first Monday in
January, and every two weeks thereafter, these five children should meet with
Uncle George in grandpa's library, and take make-believe trips with him.
If any of the older members wanted to attend, they would be expected to
observe a decorous silence.   Aunt Mary suggested that, since there were five
children, they should call themselves the " Quintet Club," and the meetings
be known as the " Travels of the Quintet Club."   But as this suggestion had
a sound of " red tape " about it, it was not adopted; but they often called
themselves " the club."   Uncle George thought that, if they met regularly
every two weeks, by spring they would be able to talk about the most interesting objects to be seen in a real tour around the world.

It was now growing late, and so, after announcing that their first visit
would be to the British Isles, the teams were brought to the door, and the
visitors departed for their homes ; the older children forming many good
resolutions as to being prepared for the first meeting.

CHAPTER II.

THE BRITISH ISLANDS.

THE TIME finally came for the first meeting of the club. The members felt a little uneasy about the preparations they had been able to make, which varied according to the mental traits of the various members. To do them justice, we must remember that it was the holidays, and we all know they had a good deal to distract their attention. Still, they had all made an effort. Willie had devoted considerable time to the encyclopedia, but, as he told his brother, he "couldn't get head or tail to it;" and so, getting a big note-book and a pencil, he concluded to await developments. Burt had gone at the matter more wisely; he had better ideas as to what was wanted, and had really tried to be prepared, the only trouble being, as he found out later, that he was making too hard work of it, and he felt a little discouraged as the first Monday in January approached. Nettie and Ida had promised themselves every day that the next day they would "study up." But in this case the "next" day succeeded in keeping one day ahead until Monday was upon them. Then they had made a vigorous effort for an hour or two, when they concluded that they had "just done all Uncle George can expect." Henry had coaxed his father and mother to tell him stories about various English kings and queens. This was fun for Henry, but some work for his parents; and we wouldn't care to vouch for the historical accuracy of all that his father told him, especially when he wanted to read the evening paper.

But the club was promptly on hand when the time came. The boys rode their ponies, and Mr. Scott's coachman drove the children over. Uncle George was waiting, and the library had been made ready especially for them. As Uncle George believed in moving on time, they were soon seated around the long study table and ready to begin, though by this time Henry had serious doubts whether this was not some sort of a school; and if so, he didn't know but he could employ himself to better advantage down with

QUEEN VICTORIA.
(CORONATION DAY.)

Aunt Mary. But as his uncle gave him a pleasant smile, and as the others didn't seem to be alarmed, he concluded he would stay awhile anyway.

"Now, children," commenced Uncle George, "I want to make these trips interesting and profitable to you. You must all feel free to ask questions, especially if you don't understand what I say. It is not my wish to make you study hard." (Several members of the club felt greatly relieved at this point.) "My aim is simply to have a pleasant talk about the principal objects and places of interest we would see in a real trip; and, of course, interesting bits of information that we can pick up will be gladly received. You can all see that we can only talk about a few of the many places we could describe; for to undertake to talk about all the interesting sights to be seen would require a good deal more time than we can give to it.

"Now," continued Uncle George, "suppose you had spent about a week on one of the big steamers I was telling you about the other night, you would be very glad to catch sight of land once more. In our present trip the first land we see after losing sight of America is Ireland. Burt, you open that large atlas and turn to Ireland."

Burt made haste to comply, and Uncle George continued:

"Now we are supposed to be steaming along the southern coast, and with a good field-glass in hand, we notice that, though the shore seems to be rocky, the greenest of grass is growing wherever there is the least chance."

"And I suppose that is why Ireland is called the Emerald Isle," said Willie. "But, uncle, what makes the grass so green and the leaves on the trees so bright?"

"Well," said his uncle, "I am glad to note that question, for it gives me a chance to try an experiment. In this case I am not going to explain it at once, but I am going to assign it to some one of you to make a special study thereon, and report at the next meeting. And so, Burt, I want you to make a little report about the climate of Western Europe at the next meeting. I don't want you to make a very long report," he added, noting the rather alarmed look on Burt's face. "You see, I want to make you observant travelers; and the only way to do so is to take note of just such questions as this, and try and understand them. But now let us return to our travels. As we want to take a trip through Ireland, we will stop at Queenstown; and here is a picture of the harbor," and Uncle George opened one of the large books.

2

"But, uncle," said Nettie, "the name under that picture is the 'Cove of Cork.'"

"So it is," said her uncle, "but the explanation is very simple. That used to be the name of the place, but in honor of a visit from Queen Victoria the name was changed to Queenstown. You must notice the harbor. It is one of the best in the world. You see the river—by the way, Burt, what river is it?"

COVE OF CORK.

"The River Lee," said Burt, glancing at the atlas.

"Yes, the River Lee widens out into a great harbor, which is almost land-locked, as they say—that is, the land closes in again so that only a narrow passage leads to the ocean; and the result is a harbor said to be the finest in Europe."

"What are all those buildings down on the water?" asked Henry, pointing to the picture.

"They are not on the water, said his uncle. That is Spike Island, which is nothing but a great big fort. Years ago they used to keep a great many convicts here who were kept at work on the fort, and you notice a bridge leading over to another small island. There are quite a number of islands in this harbor, Queenstown itself being built on the largest one. The place is not a very important one, so we will hurry on. Here, however, is a view of the principal street. And, by the way, in the old cemetery of the town lies buried the author of the 'Burial of Sir John Moore.'"

QUEENSTOWN

"Oh, yes, I know," said Nettie——

> "Not a drum was heard, not a funeral note,
> As his corse to the rampart we hurried."

Here she suddenly stopped, as she was not quite sure of the next line, and perhaps the club didn't care for poetry. But Uncle George said that it was just such little items of information that made sight-seeing in foreign lands pleasant.

"We will take a steamer from Queenstown to Cork, which is only eleven miles up the river" (here Burt pointed out the exact location on the map), "and it is a very pleasant ride. There is just the right combination of winding river, lofty hills, interspersed with green, park-like fields, to make it thoroughly enjoyable. There is a railroad skirting either shore, and the river is alive with all sorts of water craft. At last we come to Cork," and as he spoke Uncle George turned the page of the album he held in his hand, and passed it around for the club to examine.

CORK.

"And, uncle," said Henry, whose face wore the puzzled look that small boys sometimes have when they are wrestling with big ideas, "do they make corks there?"

The club indulged in a laugh, but Uncle George said he was glad to notice the question, and explained that the name of the city was derived from an old Irish word meaning "the Marsh."

"Now, in this town there are a good many interesting places to see. It is a very old town, and has a cathedral noted for its chime of bells. It is the Cathedral of St. Ann's Shandon. The steeple would attract our attention anywhere; it is faced with gray stones on three sides, and red on the other. Every traveler wants to hear its chime of bells. Poets have sung of the

'———bells of Shandon
That sound so grand on
The pleasant waters
Of the River Lee.'

"This is the first cathedral," he continued, "that I shall point out to you; but a traveler in Europe soon learns that there is nothing better worth seeing than the great cathedrals. Some of them are many centuries old, and have most interesting memories connected with them. We will try, by and by, to learn something about the different styles of architecture, and so really enjoy visiting these great churches."

SHANDON ON THE LEE.

"Cork has a history extending through more than twelve centuries. Long before Columbus discovered America it was an important town, and, as we would expect, a good many places in its immediate vicinity have most charming stories connected with them; for time will just as naturally throw around old places and old ruins legendary stories as nature will clothe them with moss."

"Tell us a story, please, uncle," said Henry. And we are not sure but if the matter had been put to vote other members of the club would have decided in favor of a story.

"I hardly think it best to do that," said his uncle with a pleasant smile; "but, as a compromise, we will talk about the 'Blarney Stone.' The people of Ireland, you know, are celebrated the world over for their ready wit; and, whether right or wrong, those in the vicinity of Cork are supposed to be especially favored in this matter. Now in this famous Castle of Blarney, some five miles from Cork, there is a stone, and it is said that whoever kisses it becomes possessed of this ready wit. There is an old poem which thus describes it:

'There is a stone there '
That whoever kisses,
Oh! he never misses
To grow eloquent.'

BLARNEY CASTLE.

"And as such he is

'To be let alone!
Don't hope to hinder him,
Or to bewilder him;
Sure, he is a pilgrim
From the Blarney Stone.' "

There was a general desire on the part of the club to know whether Uncle George had embraced this magic stone; but on that point he preserved a discreet silence.

"If we want to see beautiful scenery," continued Mr. Adams, "we must make a trip to the lake district around Killarney. See if you can find it on the atlas." As it was not plainly marked, Burt, who by tacit consent had charge of the atlas, had some difficulty in finding it, and so his uncle pointed out the location of Killarney, which was found to be in quite the southwestern part of Ireland. "You notice from the map that that part of Ireland is quite mountainous, though we would not consider them very high mountains; and as the rain-fall in Ireland is very great, we are not surprised to know there are many small lakes and some beautiful scenery in this neighborhood

GLENGARIFF AND BANTRY BAY.

"We will take the usual line of travel from Cork, and the first point of interest we will strike will be Glengariff and Bantry Bay. This view will give us an idea of the beautiful combination of hills or mountains, islands and bays. Now, Ida, as you have been so quiet, I am going to ask you to read this account of the scenery around Glengariff," said Uncle George, taking a volume from the case and opening it where he had previously placed a mark.

Rather timidly Ida read as follows: " Picture to yourself mountains of vast proportions, pyramidal form, jagged and rounded and roughened into every variety of shape. Group together trees of varied hue, such as holly, arbutus with its cluster of white waxen blossoms, like lilies in air, myrtle, birch, ash, and oak; arrange them in the most artistic manner conceivable; erect a castle yonder, a many-windowed mansion on this rising ground, here and there an ivy-mantled cottage snugly nestled. Let tawny tinctured torrents tear along channels where foam-bubbles waltz merrily as they whirl giddily onward. Now spread out a many-miled sea surface, stud it tastefully with verdurous islands, and, to sentinel the scene, erect a martello tower on this bluff-browed rock islet around which sea-weed fondly clings. Add to this the aerial garniture of a summer sunset. Can you conceive such a picture? Well, go to Glengariff, and the lovely reality will be found to be far more transcendently beautiful than any fancy sketch of either pen or pencil."

This was a hard extract to read, but Ida acquitted herself very creditably, and the club, with the picture of Glengariff before it, thought it could understand the writer's feelings.

" To reach Killarney," continued Mr. Adams, " we will take what they call a jaunting car."

" What kind of a car is that? " asked Willie.

" Well, in Ireland large sections of country can only be seen by taking some kind of a coach. The jaunting car is distinctively an Irish mode of conveyance. The outside jaunting car, which is the most common form, is a two-wheeled vehicle, with a seat along each side; the passengers sit back to back, and face outwards. Without stopping to describe this journey we will pass at once to Killarney. These celebrated lakes are surrounded on all sides by hills, which are clothed with forests of evergreen trees, plentifully interspersed with arbutus. And this tree, by the way, has most beautiful blossoms not unlike lilies of the valley, and it will take root and grow where there is almost no soil—out of the very clefts of the rock. You must try and imagine how very beautiful is the scene in the fall of the year around such a body of water as this," said Mr. Adams, at the same time turning the pages of the album he held in his hand.

" This is a view on the upper lake. The mountains in the background are the Magillicuddy Reeks; they are the highest in Ireland, though their highest peak is only about half as high as Mount Washington in our own country. The Lakes of Killarney are three in number—the Lower, Middle, and Upper Lakes—and the scenery of this whole basin is very beautiful. The people who live in the neighborhood profess to believe that at times they can see, way down under the water, submerged houses, and so have a

MAGILLICUDDY REEKS.

story to account for them. They tell of a magic fountain which was closed by a stone: just roll the stone to one side, and the flow would commence. This was a great trysting place for lovers. One night an unfortunate couple, after starting the well to flowing, were lulled to sleep by the music of the flow; and so the fountain flowed on through the night, and by morning the entire vale was submerged. Such is the story," concluded Uncle George, " but you need not believe it unless you want to."

"Another very lovely spot is what is called the ' Meeting of the Waters.' The channel connecting the Upper and Middle Lakes is about three miles long and forty feet to forty rods in width. This view is taken just at the entrance to the Middle Lake. Notice how thickly wooded it is on either side. There are mountains in the background, and at one place the mountain rises right from the very side of the channel. The peak is one great

bare rock, inaccessible from below. It is known as the Eagle's Nest, and is
noted for its echo. Our guide at that point blew his bugle, and the echo
threw the sound back to us nearly a dozen times. Sometimes it would be
loud and without interval, and then fainter and fainter; then, after a sudden
pause, again arising as if from some distant glen; then insensibly dying
away."

MEETING OF THE WATERS.

"But, uncle, what makes it do that way?" said Henry. But Uncle
George only smiled, and told him to ask his father when he got a chance to
explain to him about the echo.

"The middle lake is separated from the lower lake by a peninsula, which
is laid out as a park. As it is the private property of the Herbert family, if
we want to enjoy the beauties of the scene, we must pay an admission fee.
But it is well worth the price, since by this means we can examine the beautiful group of ruins of Muckross Abbey."

"What is an abbey?" asked Henry.

"An abbey means the buildings devoted to the use of a religious society.
And so it includes both monasteries and nunneries, or convents. But as
often used, it means only the church of such a society. The view here shown
is that of the church. Now that church is supposed to have been built nearly

six hundred years ago. Just think what stories these old walls could tell if they could only speak. In the court are buried many of the old Irish kings."

" Kings!" exclaimed Nettie in surprise.

MUCKROSS ABBEY.

" Why, yes," said Uncle George. " In the good 'ould' times that the histories speak of, Ireland was divided into several kingdoms. We are supposed to be in what was at one time the 'Kingdom of Kerry.' The traveler in Ireland," he resumed, after a thoughtful pause, " soon discovers that ruins such as those shown here are not the only ones; in a true sense the people of Ireland are themselves a ruin. But we must not stop to moralize after this fashion."

There was a mystified expression on the faces of more than one member of the club at Uncle George's last remark, but he made no explanation. Turning the pages of the album, he remarked that he would present them but one more view of Killarney, since they must be hurrying along.

"This," said he, "is a view of one of several water-falls in this vicinity. The volume of water is not great, nor the fall very high; but the surroundings are so exquisite that it is justly praised. Near here is a locality where

DERRYCUNNIHY CASCADE.

you have a splendid view of the whole section. I have here a book of poems from which I want to read a little extract, for it beautifully describes a similar scene:

> From the steep promontory gazed
> The stranger, raptured and amazed,
> And ' What a scene were here,' he cried,
> ' For princely pomp or churchman's pride!
> On this bold brow a lordly tower,
> In that soft vale a lady's bower;
> On yonder meadow, far away,
> The turrets of a cloister gray.
> How blithely might the bugle-horn
> Chide on the lake the lingering morn!

How sweet, at eve, the lover's lute
Chime when the groves were still and mute;
And when the midnight moon should lave
Her forehead in the silver wave,
How solemn on the ear would come
The holy matin's distant hum,
While the deep peal's commanding tone
Should wake, in yonder islet lone,
A sainted hermit from his cell
To drop a bead at every knell.'

"Now, we will suppose that we have taken our last look at Killarney, and we will hurry on. I am going to take you to Scotland next. Though as we

FOUR COURTS, DUBLIN.

pass through Dublin, we must take a few hours' walk through its streets. Here is one of the most striking views of the city. Dublin, you now, is the capital of Ireland. The history of this town can be carried back to a time preceding the birth of Christ, and it has had a very varied history. The river—who can tell me what river it is?"

Some of the club thought it was the Shannon, but others said it was the Liffey, which was soon found to be correct, as the Shannon was in Western Ireland.

"The river flows right through the city; there are nine bridges connecting the two parts. Two of the bridges can be seen in the picture."

"The river seems to be quite narrow," said Burt, thoughtfully.

"It is not very wide, a little over two hundred feet is all; but a few squares further down it suddenly expands into a fine bay. Trinity College, Dublin, is justly celebrated as a seat of learning, and some very eminent men were scholars here. One was Edmund Burke, and, as you have all studied history, you do not need to be told how good a friend he was to this country in the Revolutionary days. A statue to his memory stands only a few squares from the bridge shown in the picture, and close to it is the statue of another illustrious Irishman—Oliver Goldsmith. Can any of you tell me anything he wrote?"

"I think," said Nettie, hesitatingly, "that he wrote the 'Deserted Village,' commencing:

> Sweet Auburn! loveliest village of the plain,
> Where health and plenty cheered the laboring swain.

"You see, we had that in our grammar lesson," she added, "and so I remember it."

"The trip we have taken through Ireland," said Uncle George, "is a flying one often taken by tourists who can devote but a few days to their visit. It gives them a chance to see something of Irish life and scenery at very little expense of time and money. Now I hope you will remember the general outline; and whenever you have occasion to read or study about Ireland, it may seem more real to you on account of this little trip you are supposed to have taken through a part of the island.

"Now in this book" (taking up another of the albums) "I have some views of Scotland. We are supposed to have gone direct by rail from Dublin to Belfast, and thence by steamer to Glasgow.

"Here is a view of Glasgow. You could tell from it that it is one of the busy, growing, pushing-ahead sort of places. Within the present century its population has increased from less than one hundred thousand to more than half a million. It is the greatest center of ship-building in the world; and the inhabitants have displayed a great deal of energy in building up their city, and in improving the navigation of the river. They have dredged out the bottom of the river, so that the great steel war-ships now sail where the

VIEW OF GLASGOW.

33

people could wade with safety comparatively few years ago. By the way, Burt, you must hunt up the map of Scotland, point out Glasgow, and tell us what river this is."

In a very short time Burt had pointed out the location of the city, and announced that it was the River Clyde.

"The name Clyde," continued Mr. Adams, "is supposed to be derived from a word meaning 'far-heard' or 'powerful.' There are three water-falls, not very far apart, about twenty-five miles from Glasgow, which, when the river is in flood, can be heard for a long distance—not that they are so high, but the high ravine and rocky side of the wall make the echo very . distinct."

"The way it was at that other place," said Henry, rather indefi-nitely, thinking of the Eagle's Nest at Killarney.

"Yes," said his uncle, "on the same principles. And here is a view of the principal fall, called Corra Linn. There are three separate falls here, eighty feet in all. There is a verse of an old ballad which gives a traveler's address to the Clyde:

CORRA LINN.

O roaring Clyde, ye roar ower loud,
Your streams seem wonder strang:
Mak me your prey as I come back,
But spare me as I gang.

"The whole course of the Clyde, and especially the upper portion of it, is historic ground for the people of Scotland. Have any of you ever heard of Wallace?"

Though several had heard of him, there was a general curiosity to know what he had to do with the Clyde.

"Well, some six centuries ago, though England and Scotland were separate countries, there was a great struggle going on between them. At that time the king of England was Edward I., an ambitious man, who used every artifice in his power to extend his sway over Scotland; and unfortunately, near the end of the thirteenth century, Scotland was divided by contending factions, and so, for the time being, England had it all her own way. Wallace was one of those national heroes who, amidst the great difficulties, finally succeeded in

BOTHWELL CASTLE.

rousing the national spirit and regaining, to a large extent, the liberties of his people. A vast amount of tradition and romance has gathered about his name, and it is almost impossible to tell what is truth and what is fiction. But the principal scene of his exploits was along the upper Clyde. Of nearly every place some story is told about what Wallace did there. Here, for instance, are the ruins of Bothwell Castle, but a few miles from Glasgow. This was built by the English to be a stronghold during the troublous times we have just mentioned. Wallace and his force hid themselves in the forests along the river, and were ever ready to pounce on any stray force of English. And the early histories are full of his wonderful exploits.

VIEWS IN STAFFA.

"But if we were to stop and talk all about Wallace, we will take up all the evening, so we will come back to Glasgow and start on our travels once more. There are two very interesting places on the western coast of Scotland. Nearly every traveler pays them a visit. They are the Islands of Staffa and Iona. You have all of you heard of Fingal's Cave?"

3

"Why yes," said Nettie, "I know just how the picture looks in the geography."

"Well," said her uncle, "here is a group of four views in the vicinity of the cave. Now this cave is a most wonderful scene. You notice in all the views the appearance of columns. Those are all natural columns of what our geologists call basalt."

"But what is basalt, and what makes it take that form, uncle?" asked Willie.

"I am afraid I cannot explain in a few words," said Uncle George, "but I can give you an idea, and you can look it up at your leisure. You all know what lava is. Well, basalt is a lava rock—that is, lava cooled under pressure. As it gradually cools it contracts, but the outer surface becomes solidified first; hence the cooling mass tends to split, and the strain being uniform, the fractures are uniform; hence the tendency is to split into these six-sided prisms you see here. But now you must study this up" (speaking more especially to the boys). "You see, the rest of the club is not particularly interested in this matter.

"The cave itself is about sixty feet high, and about two hundred feet long; forty feet wide at the entrance, gradually diminishing to about twenty-two feet at the further end. The sea never entirely leaves the cave. The water is of a beautiful green color, and with its reflected light it lights up the whole interior. The waves, as they ebb and flow, or dash wildly in, cause a gentle musical murmur or resounding roar, the

Diapason of the deep,

as Scott calls it.

> That mighty surge that ebbs and swells,
> And still, between each awful pause,
> From the high vault an answer draws,
> In varied tone, prolonged and high,
> That mocks the organ's melody.

"The old native name, by the way, was the 'musical cave.' It has often been likened to a cathedral.

> ———as to shame the temples decked
> By skill of earthly architect,
> Nature herself, it seemed, would raise
> A minster to her Maker's praise!

"Take it all together, this is one of the most interesting points we could visit. But while we have been looking at the picture, have you, Burt, found on the map just where this island of Staffa is?"

RUINS OF IONA CATHEDRAL.

But Burt had already found that it was one of the Hebrides, to the west of Scotland, and so Uncle George continued:

"You see, to the south of Staffa, about eight miles distance, a second small island marked Iona. This is another interesting spot where all tourists stop; but the interest here is altogether historical. This was a great center of religious culture. In the middle of the sixth century, twelve hundred years ago, Saint Columba, an Irish saint, settled on this little island and made it his headquarters.

A most famous monastery was erected; but the ruins shown in this cut do
not belong to that, but to a far later time.   Iona became a sort of Jerusalem
for all these northern regions.   The poets speak of

Old Iona's holy fane,

And it is interesting to pour over the old records of this monastery.   During
the time of the ravages of the Northmen it was sacked, and the abbot and

TOMBS OF THE KINGS, IONA.

fifteen of the monks were murdered.   About the twelfth century prosperity
returned to Iona.   It became noted as a place of learning.   A perpetual stream
of travelers seem to have flowed backwards and forwards of those thirsting
for its literary treasures.   They came not only from Ireland and England,
but from the continent of Europe as well.   It was regarded as such a holy
place that people of distinction were carried thither for burial, so we find here ·
the oldest cemetery in Scotland.   Lately these graves, or rather tombstones,
have been arranged in something like order.   Here, for instance, is seen the

tombs of the kings. More than forty kings of various races—Scottish, Irish, Norwegian, and even French—are said to have been buried on this island. You notice carvings in the stone; they are representations of swords, ships, armorial bearings, and warriors. You can well see what an interesting place this little island off the coast of Scotland is. It was the Athens and Mecca both of all this northern region."

Uncle George had unconsciously lapsed into language rather hard for all of the club to understand. Henry was decidedly puzzled to know what his uncle meant when he said Iona was both Athens and Mecca; and we are not sure that the older members could have fully explained it to him. In fact, Uncle George seemed suddenly to recollect himself, and smiled as he turned to another subject.

"Scotland is especially noted for its glen scenery."

"What kind of scenery, uncle?" exclaimed Burt, not waiting for the explanation which his uncle was about to give.

"Why, a glen is a long narrow valley. They often inclose a lake, or a *loch*, as they call them in Scotland. The glens of Scotland are among the most beautiful in the world. You see, everything is combined to form a beautiful picture. The forests show a great variety of foliage; the waters change from lake to rushing torrent or foaming water-fall; the hills are a constant alternation of light and shade. Find Oban, Burt."

Burt pointed it out on the western shore.

"Oban is the great gathering point for tourists in the Western Highlands, and there we will return after our excursion to Staffa and Iona. You notice Loch Awe to the south of Oban. This whole section around this loch was the home of the MacGregor Clan, of which Rob Roy was the famous chieftain. Some of you, perhaps, have read the novel by that name."

None of the club had, but several mentally resolved to look it up.

"But, uncle," said Burt, "you just spoke about the MacGregor Clan, and I have read before about the clans of Scotland. What are they, anyway?"

After a thoughtful pause Uncle George said:

"Well, Burt, a good deal of time could be spent in answering your question. Once on a time the people were all in what we call a tribal state. You know in the Bible we read about the tribes of the Jews, and in ancient history you read of the Greek and Latin tribes; and when Rome was a civilized country, all Europe was still occupied by tribes. Well, these clans of

Scotland were nothing but the old tribes still keeping up old customs. They had their chiefs, and carried to a ridiculous extent their devotion to tribe and chieftain.

"We must not leave Oban without visiting the Castle of Dunstaffnage, shown in this cut, located only a few miles to the northeast of Oban, placed at the very entrance of Loch Etive. This is one of the most interesting spots in the history of Scotland. That ruined castle was once the seat of

DUNSTAFFNAGE CASTLE.

government of the Scots from the end of the fifth to the middle of the ninth century, before they conquered the Picts, after which they moved their capital. Here was kept the rough-hewn block of red sandstone on which their kings were crowned, and which was carried to England by Edward I., and placed beneath the Coronation Chair in Westminster Abbey, where it is still to be seen."

"Who were the Picts, and what was the difference between them and the Scots?" asked Nettie.

"You who have read history," said her uncle, in answer to her question, "know that in old Roman times all that part of Scotland lying to the north

of a line connecting the Firths of Forth and Clyde "—indicating it on the
map that Burt held in his hand—"was known as Caledonia. Afterward these
Caledonians were known as the Picts, and from them the country was called
Pictland. The Scots were an invading tribe that came originally from
Ireland and settled in the West Highlands. They finally conquered the
Picts, and changed the name of the country to Scotland."

"So the Scotch are really Irish, are they?" exclaimed Nettie.

"Well, hardly that," said her uncle with a laugh, in which the club joined,
"though there is a great deal of resemblance between the ·inhabitants of
Northern Ireland and Scotland. They both belong to the Gallic division of
the Celtic branch of the Aryan people; but we are getting beyond our depth,
and must return. You see, though, how much there is to learn in a trip of
this kind.

"What is known as the 'Great Glen' of Scotland extends from Loch
Linnhe (Oban is on Loch Linnhe, you know) to Moray Firth on the other
shore. This is a singular depression. If Scotland were to sink just a little
into the sea, a long narrow strait would occupy this valley, and what is now
the Northern Highlands of Scotland would be a great island. The long
ravine is bounded on either side by lofty hills, and is occupied by a series of
narrow lakes. . You notice there is a canal the whole length. Only about
one-third of the way had to be excavated; the rest of the way nature had
already prepared by means of the lakes we have just mentioned and navigable
rivers. A trip through the canal is a very interesting one, as it gives us a
chance to see all sorts of Scottish scenery.

"In our next view is to be seen the most charming bit of scenery on the
whole route. It is the ruined castle of Invergarry. It was burned in 1746
by the 'butcher' Cumberland. . I will tell you about him in just a little
while," he added, noting the inquiring look on the face of several of the club.

"The shell of the old castle is beautifully situated on a rocky knoll,
dense foliage all about it, and right in front is Loche Oich. If you stop to
approach the castle, your attention would be arrested by a singular monument
placed over a spring. The spring is called the 'Well of Seven Heads.' The
monument consists of seven stone heads, surmounting a pyramid. The story
told about them is that two sons of an influential family were sent to France
to be educated. Their father died, and the management of their estate was
left in the hands of seven cousins. They liked their job so well that when

the rightful heirs returned they murdered them. But dire vengeance overtook them. The old bard of the family obtained help, and slew them. Not the finest kind of a story to tell in connection with such beautiful scenery, is it?

" Before we pass out of the glen, when we get within six miles of Inverness, we pass an historical spot—that is the battle-field of Culloden. Did you ever hear of it?"

INVERGARRY CASTLE.

Nettie, who seemed to be the one who could recall many little bits of poetry, suggested that it was mentioned in " Lochiel's Warnings."

" That's right," said Uncle George.

——— Culloden's dread echo shall ring
With the bloodhounds that bark for thy fugitive king.

" Here was where ' Crested Lochiel, the peerless in might,' gathered the clans of Culloden, but was overthrown in battle with the English forces, led by the Duke of Cumberland. And here is where the latter got his title of ' butcher' that I said I would talk about a moment ago."

" Do you mean he was the one that burned that nice looking castle?" inquired Henry, pointing to the castle of Invergarry.

"The same," said his uncle. "You that have read history know that Charles Edward, the 'young Pretender,' as he was called, made an attempt to gain the crown of England in 1745. The clans of Scotland supported his claims. Their power was broken in this battle of Culloden. After the battle the English behaved with great severity toward the wounded and prisoners. But we must hurry along, and we will go directly to Edinburgh on the eastern shore.

EDINBURGH CASTLE.

"Edinburgh was the old capital of Scotland, and, of course, we could spend a great deal of time here; but we will content ourselves with just one view. Here is the famous castle of Edinburgh. You see it is upon a hill nearly three hundred feet above the valley. The hill is very precipitous on three sides. Sometimes the kings of Scotland lived in the castle, and sometimes they were imprisoned there by their powerful barons. In this castle is to be seen the regalia, or, as they are called, the honors of Scotland. They consist of the crown, scepter, sword of state, and Lord-Treasurer's rod of office. There is an interesting story about these 'honors.' When James VI. of Scotland became James I. of England, Scotland refused to let the regalia be carried to London; and for fear that this would happen they were concealed in a vault in a church. Then, long afterward, they were brought to the castle, put in a strong oaken chest, and locked up in a room which was never opened. Their very existence was forgotten, though now and then some national bard would sing about:

> The steep and iron-belted rock
> Where trusted lie the monarchy's lost gems—
> The scepter, sword, and crown—that graced the brows
> Since Father Fergus, of a hundred kings.

"But in 1817 a general desire rose to find them, and a committee, including Sir Walter Scott, proceeded to the spot. The kings' smith was commanded to force open the great chest, the keys of which had been sought for in vain. You can well imagine how pleased they all were, and how pleased all Scotland was, to find these precious 'honors' uninjured after their long concealment of nearly two centuries.

"Now, as we still want to talk about England and Wales, we must hurry along. We will suppose that we are back to Dublin, and that we are not going to Scotland, but to England. We will go directly to Liverpool, but will not stop there. The fact is, Liverpool is a modern city, and the traveler will not see much to remind him of foreign lands; in fact, he might well imagine himself in New York or Boston. There is one sight, however, that always impresses travelers landing in Liverpool (and you know there are a great many such, for the great majority of tourists make their first landing here), and that is the immense docks. They are really among the wonders of the world. Fifteen years ago they covered an area of nearly three hundred acres, and they have been greatly extended since. You who have been to New York or any seaport city have seen what we call docks—that is, a more or less protected basin where ships can approach the wharves, and receive or discharge their cargoes. But at Liverpool the tide rises so high that it is necessary to take some means for keeping the water on a level. So these docks are immense inclosed basins, protected by a great wall of solid masonry, running for five miles along the shore, and only entered by enormous gates.

"But, as I remarked, aside from these docks, there is but little to interest us in Liverpool. Only a few miles from Liverpool, however, we do find a city that carries us back to old times. That city is Chester. Point it out on the map, Burt; south of Liverpool, at the mouth of the River Dee."

"All these big places are on rivers, ain't they, uncle?" said Henry.

"Oh, yes, that's true," said Uncle George, "and there are a great many reasons why it should be so. All the more important cities of the world are on rivers or some important body of water. Here is a view of Chester," and as he spoke he opened still a third album.

VIEW FROM THE WALLS OF CHESTER.

"What is that it says about 'view from the walls,' uncle?" asked Nettie, referring to the title of the picture.

"I was just going to remark," continued Mr. Adams, "that Chester is one of the few examples of walled towns now remaining in England. The town is entirely surrounded by walls, though they would not be good for much as far as defense is concerned; but they do afford a fine promenade about the city. Chester carries us back to old Roman days. They built a fortified camp here, and for several hundred years it was a Roman outpost. A legion of soldiers was stationed here, and the name Chester is derived from a Latin word meaning camp. Then after the Romans left, Chester still remained an important place. A great many mementoes of Roman times, such as tombs, inscriptions, pottery, fragments of mosaic pavements, and coins, have been found. A great deal of ancient history is connected with this town which we cannot stop to talk about.

"The walls are probably the most interesting feature about Chester, though they do not reach back to the Roman period by many centuries. There are a number of gates and towers in the wall nearly all of interesting historical significance. Here are views of two of the towers. The one marked the ' Phœnix Tower ' bears this inscription : ' King Charles stood on this tower Septr. 24th, 1645, and saw his army defeated on Rowton Moor.'

PHŒNIX TOWER.

WATER TOWER.

And in connection with that inscription I would say that Chester was one of the towns that stood up for Charles I. in his quarrel with his Parliament."

"And he got his head cut off, too," said Henry, recalling a story he had coaxed out of his father only the night before. "I bet he felt bad when he saw his soldiers whipped," he added.

"Undoubtedly he did," said Uncle George, "but he couldn't blame any one but himself for his troubles. Now from Chester we can take a little run

into North Wales. You notice on the map which Burt holds in his hand the Island of Anglesey. It is separated from the mainland of Wales by a narrow strait. Standing on its shores you would never think it was really an arm of the sea; you would surely call it a river. The channel is narrow and winding; the banks are quite steep, and often wooded to the very shore. A good deal of history is connected with the shores of this strait. It was here that the Romans met with the fiercest resistance; and the old historian Tacitus gives an interesting account of the attack on the Island of *Mona*, as it was called by them. In his description he tells about the Druid priests urging on the natives to battle."

MENAI SUSPENSION BRIDGE.

"There," said Willie, "I saw something about those Druids, the other day, in the encyclopedia, and I was going to ask you about them."

"I will only take time now to say that the priests of all savage people tend to form a closely connected body, and among quite a number of the people of Western Europe this body of priests was known as Druids. Long after Roman times the Saxon kings of England fought many desperate battles along these shores. Here is a picture that will give you an idea of the scenery along the strait. You notice a suspension bridge. But a short distance below this bridge there is another, not quite so nice looking, but generally regarded as a more wonderful piece of work, called the Tubular

Bridge. Two immense iron tubes are stretched across the straits, supported by a tower in the center of the strait.

"Now we will go back to Chester. It is only a few hours' ride by railway, and let us look at some of the English water scenery. The lake district of England is away up in the northwestern part. Here we have a view of the

DERWENTWATER.

most noted lake, Derwentwater. Notice the big hills surrounding it. And, by the way, all the hills or mountains, as they might be called in this district, have a wonderful story to tell if we only know how to question them right."

"What do you mean, uncle?" asked Henry, who hardly knew what to make of his uncle's words.

"Why, I mean this, Henry, if we only knew how to explain everything we see in connection with the mountains, we will come upon quite an interesting period in the early history of the world. Because once on a time this whole section must have been thickly studded with volcanoes. There must have been tremendous eruptions of lava; vast quantities of ashes and broken stones were also poured out. Some of the hills that overlook this lake are simply lava ridges which, in the long lapse of ages, have been clothed with vegetation. So you see how much is to be learned if we only know how to observe.

"Right on the edge of this lake there is a water-fall which is celebrated, not for the amount of water or height of fall, but for what the poet Southey has written about it. That is the Fall of Lodore."

As he said this, Uncle George picked up a book, opened it, and asked Ida to read a verse he pointed out. Ida read as follows :

And thumping and plumping and
    bumping and jumping,
And dashing and flashing and splash-
    ing and clashing,
And so never ending, but always de-
    scending,
Sounds and motions forever and ever
    are blending
All at once and all o'er with a mighty
    uproar ;
And this way the water comes down at
    Lodore.

FALLS OF LODORE.

"That is a very fine piece of writing," said Uncle George, "but it is hardly true of the fall itself, unless you happen there shortly after a big rain, otherwise it is rather a tame sight.

"As for English scenes proper, the best course is to select various views without regard to the order in which they occur.

"I want to talk to you about Centerbury Cathedral. There are other cathedrals in England more imposing, perhaps; but none have the historical interest that attaches itself to Canterbury. This also was an important place even in Roman times."

" Uncle," said Nettie, " I wanted to ask you once before just what you meant by Roman times."

" Why, when the Romans held Great Britain," exclaimed Burt, when he stopped, rather confused, to think he had undertaken to answer the question. But his uncle said that was all right, and asked him to be a little more definite in his reply.

CANTERBURY CATHEDRAL.

" Well," said Burt, " I read in Hume's history how the Romans, led by Cæsar, invaded Britain about 55 B. C., but how Agricola was the general who finally conquered the island, and then when Rome began to fall to pieces they abandoned it about 448 A. D.; and the time between these two dates must be what is meant by the Roman period."

" Very good," said Uncle George. " Well, in Roman times, as I said, Canterbury was quite a point. This importance it still maintained when the Saxons took possession of Britain. But its great importance is from a religious view. Near the end of the sixth century a band of monks, under the lead of Augustin, arrived in England, and were assigned quarters in

Canterbury. From that time until the present day it has remained the center of religious life in England. In the views I have here you see the present appearance of the cathedral and that portion of it known as 'the choir.'

THE CHOIR.

"During the Middle Ages this became a very celebrated place, owing to the martyrdom of Thomas 'a Becket. Becket was the Archbishop of Canterbury. He got into an unfortunate quarrel with Henry II., and was finally murdered by some over-zealous friends of the king.

"Now in the next view you see the place—although it has been completely remodeled since—where this cruel deed took place."

4

"I think I have read somewhere that the king had to do penance for this," said Burt.

"Oh, yes; it soon became evident that this act was not only a crime, but, politically speaking, a blunder. King Henry went barefooted to the grave, and remained there all night, besides submitting to light blows from each bishop and monk."

TRANSEPT OF THE MARTYRDOM.

"I wouldn't have done that if I had been king," said Henry. But Uncle George only smiled, and turned to another subject.

"Now," he continued, "I am going to show you views of some castles. A traveler in Europe finds a great deal to interest him in the ruined castles. They are not only picturesque ruins, but they generally have a good deal of history connected with them, going back to the old feudal times."

Burt could not forbear asking his uncle what he meant by *feudal* times;

but his uncle thought it best not to attempt to enter into an explanation, and told him to look it up; and if he could not understand it, he would explain it to him some other time. And we might add that Burt found a great deal to be learned about that subject.

FLINT CASTLE.

"Here is a view of a castle in the southwestern part of England, almost on the border of Wales. There is not so much of interest about it, though it is a fine ruin. During the wars between King Charles and his Parliament a number of battles were fought for the possession of this castle; and when the Parliamentary forces conquered, they destroyed as much of it as they well could. Near here is the Chepstow Castle, which is noted as the place of the long imprisonment of Henry Marten, one of the regicides. Can any of you tell me about the regicides?" he added, noting the inquiring look on more than one face.

No one volunteering to answer, Uncle George continued: "When King Charles 'got his head cut off,' as Henry said a minute ago, it was done, of course, under process of law. The judges who tried him and condemned him to death were afterwards called regicides, meaning king-murderers. Marten was one of them who trusted to the promises of Charles II. that he would pardon them. But, instead of so doing, he was confined in Chepstow Castle for twenty years.

WINDSOR CASTLE.

"But, talking about castles of England, we cannot do better than to visit Windsor Castle. This castle has not only a good deal of history connected with it, but is at the present day intimately connected with British royalty. It is beautifully situated. The Thames River, as you see, runs at its base, and the whole site is historic. Runnymead and Magna Charta Island are right before us. You that have read history do not need to be told how important those places are in the history of English liberty. And if you have not read about them, you will be much interested in reading any good history about the trouble between King John and his barons."

"Magna Charta," repeated Henry, "I heard something about that, but tell me a little about it now."

"Well, only just an outline then. Early in the thirteenth century John, King of England, found himself involved in disputes with his barons, the powerful nobles of England. They forced from the king what is known as the Magna Charta. It was really a treaty between the king and his people. It gave to the people the promise of freedom, justice, good government, and security from unjust taxation. This celebrated charter was signed on what has been known since as Magna Charta Island. This little picture represents the great wrath of John in having to sign the treaty. Referring to Windsor Castle again, I might say that the big

JOHN SWEARING VENGEANCE AGAINST HIS BARONS.

round tower we noticed is supposed to have been built by William the Conqueror. Here is a little piece that I want Ida to read for us."

Ida read as follows: "The history of Windsor Castle is, to a great extent, the history of England. * * * In its walls our monarchs have dwelt in uninterrupted succession since the days of Henry Beauclerc; in its chambers no little of their life's drama has been played. Courtiers have intrigued or plotted: this one has been raised to sudden favor, that dismissed to disgrace or to the headsman's ax. Princes have been born, been wedded, and died: not a few of our kings and their kindred rest in the vaults of its chapel. There have been many other royal houses in their time, but all have had their day. The Tower of London is but a barrack for soldiers and a store-house for arms; the Royal Palace of Westminster but a name; St. James is practically untenanted save by dependents; Kensington and Kew are in like condition; Sheen, Theobalds, and many more have disappeared

EXECUTION OF CHARLES THE FIRST.

or are owned by other lords: but Windsor Castle remains the historic palace of our kings, the inalienable possession of the Crown of Great Britain."

"Now that gives us an idea of the importance of Windsor Castle," said Mr. Adams; "and, as it says, many kings are buried in its vaults. Henry VIII. rests here, after his strange career, by the side of Jane Seymour; and thither was borne the body of Charles I. after his sad execution. It was taken there secretly in the dead of night."

HENRY VIII.

59

"Another class of ruins of great interest to all travelers is that of ancient abbeys."

"Like that one in Ireland," broke in Henry, thinking of Muckross Abbey at Killarney.

BEAULIEU ABBEY.

"Yes," continued Uncle George, "that is one example. England was once very plentifully supplied with abbeys, and their ruins are often very interesting. Here is a view of one in the southern part of England. What a beautiful ruin that is, all overgrown with running vines! The country round about is interesting, too. England once on a time was a very heavily wooded country. This part of the island never has been cleared up. And here used to be the royal hunting grounds. Here was where William Rufus, the Red King, was hunting on that fatal day that he was killed by a glancing arrow. You must look this point up in your history.

GREAT PORTAL, CROWLAND ABBEY.

"Now, I will take you to another part of England to view this ruin This is in the eastern part of England, in what is known as the Fenlands. You notice what they call The Wash on the eastern shore. The country all around is very low and marshy, so it is called the Fenlands. Within the last century it has been dyked and ditched, and so is much better than it once was. Abbeys were once very thick here. Every little piece of land more elevated than the general mass was the site of an abbey. The reason is quite obvious. Such little tracts of land were fertile and well protected. Those who fled from the world found here a quiet, safe retreat. This particular group of ruins dates from times preceding the Norman Conquest; indeed, those were the days of its greatest prosperity, and a good deal of English history is connected with it which we cannot now stop to talk about.

BISHAM ABBEY.

"It is now getting late, but I want to show you some views of English river scenery. We cannot do better than to take the Thames. The Thames from Windsor to Reading has on its banks some of the finest river scenery in the world. Groves mantle the steeper parts; they cluster thickly on the brow of the plateau, and seem to extend backward from its edge far over the uplands. In the intervals between them are grassy slopes—sometimes fields of waving grain—all diversified with scattered trees. Here and there we may see some stately mansion, or at the foot of a long slope some little village, or a larger

town with a magnificent park laid out along the river bank. The views
which we have are a fair sample of the scenes, and with them we will close our
trip for to-night."

THE THAMES AT RAY MEAD.

We do not think that Uncle George would have stopped at this point,
but Aunt Mary entered the room, and he knew that in her estimation it was
time for the club to adjourn. As he closed the book, Mr. Adams continued:

"You see, children, this is our first meeting, and we will know better
how to go about next time. We will look at some pictures of Scandinavia
and Russia two weeks from to-night. Burt, remember you must look up about

the climate of the British Isles. I hope you have enjoyed yourselves; and if you think of any questions you would like to ask about the places we have visited to-night, you must feel free to do so."

Soon after, the members of the club were on their way home, and it was the general opinion they had had a pleasant time. They certainly had learned quite a number of little facts in regard to the history and geography of the British Islands. As Ida said, "It seemed more real than what they read in the old books at school."

Ah, Ida! the trouble is not in the books, but in your feelings. One is work, the other play; and this distinction makes a wonderful difference not only with little boys and girls, but with men and women as well.

WILLIAM THE CONQUEROR.

CHAPTER III.

SCANDINAVIA AND RUSSIA.

THE middle of January approached, and the time came for the second meeting of the club, the weather was not as pleasant as before. The customary January thaw, with its usual accompaniment of slush, had come. But it was again growing cold. Old Winter, as if ashamed of his momentary weakness, was again asserting his authority. Perhaps he had sent a peremptory order to Boreas that there must be no more dallying. At any rate the north wind was getting down to business again, and the signal service gave warning that away up in Manitoba a new consignment of winter weather, fairly entitled to be called a blizzard, was on its way. But Uncle George's nephews and nieces were glad when the time came to meet again. The library was warm and light. Uncle George had been to New York on a little matter of business, but he had returned some days before; and we expect, if the truth were told, that he, too, enjoyed these evenings with the children: for, did you know that those who have experienced the trials as well as the pleasures that come with the passage of years know of nothing more pleasant than the companionship of innocent, pure-minded children?

And so we need not wonder that Uncle George's greeting was so cheery that every member of the club felt at home. Henry did not have the remotest idea of staying down with Aunt Mary this time; but, on the contrary, thought he could see better right up side of Uncle George, who certainly was glad to have the little fellow there. Mrs. Scott had accompanied the children this time, and she and Aunt Mary had ventured to seat themselves at the further end of the room. They were apparently busy with some light fancy work, but their attention was mainly centered on the children.

"Now, before we commence the evening's trip," began Uncle George, "I want Burt to tell us what he has learned about the climate of Western Europe."

"Why, I studied that point up some, uncle, but I hardly know as I understand it myself. It seems that the Gulf Stream has a good deal to do with it. We all know what that is, unless it is Henry here. But I was surprised to see it all figured out—what an immense amount of heat is carried out of the Gulf of Mexico by that current. As it passes north it gradually bends off to the east, and finally passes quite near to the shores of the British Islands and Norway—in fact, of Western Europe generally—and so the winds that blow off of the ocean on those lands I have named are warm and moist winds. Why, I read that if it were not for the Gulf Stream that England and Scotland and Ireland would be most as badly off as Labrador. But, on account of it, the myrtle blooms in Northern Ireland, and even way up in the Faroe Islands the inland waters do not freeze in winter. I think it is pretty lucky for all that country that it has our Gulf Stream."

"How big is it?" asked Willie.

"Oh, it is bigger than all the rivers of the world put together," exclaimed Burt. "I read that it was real narrow and deep where it starts, down by the Strait of Florida, but that it spreads out and loses in depth as it flows on. But some one estimated that on an average it was fifty miles wide, one thousand feet deep, and runs, or flows, four miles an hour."

"My!" exclaimed Nettie; but Henry didn't clearly understand what they were talking about.

"That is very good," said Uncle George. "You now see, Willie, why the vegetation was so green in Ireland. But we must go ahead with our work for the evening.

"Scandinavia includes the peninsula of Denmark, and that of Norway and Sweden. Here we strike a foreign land, for the language is no longer English. That will not bother us any, for the American traveler, wherever he goes, will find some one who understands English. Of late years the tide of travel has turned more and more toward this part of Europe. Some one has said that Scandinavia fills a larger place in the history of Europe than it does on the map, and that is a true saying. Did you ever hear of the vikings?"

The name had a familiar sound to several, but they couldn't quite place it, and Mr. Adams continued:

"In time long gone by the inhabitants of Scandinavia were the fiercest kind of pirates. You see from the position of their country they naturally became expert sailors, and in those early days it was not thought wrong to rob and murder foreign people. So these restless Scandinavians would organize piratical expeditions. Now, here is a picture of one of their old boats in which they made such voyages. It is surprising how far they would

ANCIENT VIKING BOAT.

venture in such boats. There was scarcely a country of Europe that did not dread them. In your history you have doubtless read how terribly England suffered by their inroads. These rovers of the sea were called vikings. Of late years we in America have taken a new interest in them, since we now know they discovered America nearly a thousand years ago."

"Why, was Columbus a viking, uncle?" asked Henry.

"Oh, no, Henry," said Uncle George. "You see Columbus simply re-discovered America. These old vikings found it, though, four hundred years before he did. But let us come back to our trip. Burt, you open the atlas at the large map of Europe."

When Burt had opened the atlas so that all could see, Mr. Adams said:

70

VIEWS IN COPENHAGEN.

" Now, Denmark will not detain us long. We will stop at Copenhagen. That is on the Island of Zealand. There is actually nothing in the country to interest us. The peninsula of Jutland is sandy and uninteresting. The islands are more attractive. Here we have a collection of views in Copenhagen. Number one is one of the old palaces now used by the Academy of Fine Arts. Two is the interior of one of their churches. Three is the university. Four is the large open square called the King's New Market. Twelve streets branch out from this square to different parts of the city. Number six is the Thorwaldsen Museum. Thorwaldsen was the greatest sculptor of Europe in his day, and Copenhagen is very proud of him. This museum is entirely given up to mementoes of him. Not shown in this view, but near the Christiansburg Palace is another great museum, which is among the most valuable in Europe. It is the 'Museum of Northern Antiquities and Ethnographic Museum.' They have there a most wonderful collection of objects illustrating every step in the various stages of civilization through which their country has passed, from the earliest times down. You will understand the importance of such a collection when you get older and learn with how much interest scholars all over the world are now studying into such questions.

"Denmark is now but a fragment of what it once was. The Faroe Islands belong to Denmark, so do Iceland and Greenland. Norway used to belong to it. In fact, once on a time Denmark just about ruled all Europe. That was in the days of King Canute, when the British Islands formed a part of his possessions. When you get older and read 'Hamlet,' you will see how Shakespeare refers to that old time, when the king says:

> And England, if my love thou hold'st at aught,
> As my great power thereof may give thee sense,
> Since yet thy cicatrice looks raw and red
> After the Danish sword, and thy free awe
> Pays homage to us ———.

"And we might remark that Elsinore, the scene of 'Hamlet,' is but two hours ride from Copenhagen, and there the guides will show you the 'grave of Hamlet' and the 'brook of Ophelia.' It is needless to add that these are entirely spurious; but, as the tourists keep asking for such things, they kindly supplied the long-felt want."

5

"How long ago was it that Denmark was so prosperous, uncle?" asked Willie.

"King Canute reigned early in the eleventh century; and, by the way, here is a picture of this king, and a good story is told of him. His courtiers, to flatter him, told him that the very winds and waves would obey his voice. To rebuke them he caused his chair to be placed where the tides would

CANUTE THE GREAT AND HIS COURTIERS.

overflow it. When the water came crawling up, and got unpleasantly near him, he commanded it to retire. This, of course, had no effect on the water; and then the king reminded his courtiers of their foolish words, and told them that God was the only real king. It is said that he never wore a crown after that event.

"From Copenhagen we will start for Norway, going direct to Christiana. And here is a view of the city. Have you found it, Burt?—almost north from Copenhagen, at the head of Bohus Bay."

But Burt had already pointed it out.

"This is the capital of Norway, and is very pleasantly situated. You see the fiord is dotted with islands; the hills round about are covered with firs; that little river—the Agerselv—intersects the city. The Norwegian Parliament meets here; and should you want to study about the Viking Age, you will find a splendid collection at this place of their arms and implements. Christiana is well worth a visit from the tourist, though we cannot agree with the natives—and, by the way, you cannot find a people who think more of their country—when they calmly assert that it is a finer city than Paris.

CHRISTIANA.

"Uncle, I wanted to ask you what is a fiord," broke in Henry.

"Well, you look at that map of Norway that Burt has, Henry, and don't you see how very irregular—all notched, so to speak—the coast is? Those are narrow little valleys running in from the sea, and the sea-water, generally quite deep, covers the bottom. The native name for these is fiord, and sometimes they extend a long ways inland. I may say that some of the finest scenery in the world is to be seen along the coast of Norway.

"Now, I want to show you one more Norwegian city, and so will take one on the western coast—that is Bergen. There is a fine harbor here, and you notice the hills behind the city. It is said that there is no getting out

of Bergen on the east or north, except by going right straight up, the hills
are so very steep. But toward the south they are not so steep, and the road
is bordered for miles with pretty country houses of wood, brightly painted
and curiously carved, with pretty summer homes perched among the trees.
If we should follow along the coast, we come upon a wooded country with

BERGEN.

stony hills, meadows strewn with bowlders, and we would not go far before
we would come upon some fiord. Bergen was for a long while one of the
principal cities of the Hanseatic League."

"I am glad you mentioned that, uncle; I wanted to find out something
about that league," said Burt.

"The Hanseatic League was an association of cities along the Baltic and in Northern Europe generally. They were united for the purpose of trade. It accomplished a wonderful work in civilizing Northern Europe, making all sections of Europe acquainted with each other, and suppressing piracy. It became very powerful, too. In the latter part of the fifteenth century it waged war, with success, against England. It did for Northern Europe what

HANSEATIC SHIP.

the Phœnicians did for the Mediterranean region. You see, trade and commerce have done more to make our lives on the earth pleasant than all the wars put together. By the way, I have here a picture of one of the vessels of this league. For several centuries it was very powerful in the affairs of Northern Europe; and Bergen, as I said, was one of its principal cities.

"Now, we are not through with Norway, but I am going to show you some Swedish views. You, of course, know that Sweden and Norway are now united. The union, however, is a very loose one. It is what they call a personal union—that is to say, they have the same king, but each country is entirely independent as far as making its own laws and self-government is concerned. Here is a view of Stockholm; that, you know, is the capital of Sweden. You find it on the map, right on the eastern side of Sweden, at the junction of Lake Malar with the Baltic.

STOCKHOLM.

"The way tourists generally approach Stockholm it appears very beautiful and strangely varied. Lake Malar is thickly dotted with islands. I have seen that there are some thirteen hundred of them. The city is built partly on these islands, and for that reason is sometimes called the 'Venice of the North.' When we talk about the real Venice, you will see why Stockholm is so named." (This last was in answer to an inquiring look from Henry.) "The view before us is that of the central island, Staden. You see there are excellent harbors on both the Malar and Baltic sides of the city, and so there is a constant hurrying to and fro of ocean-bound ships and steamers, loading and unloading, and bound for various parts of the world.

"In the background of the center of this picture you notice a prominent building, with a cupola on top. Well, that is the Royal Palace, and here is another view of the same building, which is really a magnificent building.

"The builders had one of the most beautiful sites in all Europe to build upon, and took excellent advantage of it. There are over five hundred rooms in the palace, not counting the kitchens and cellars, and some of the rooms are simply magnificent. The throne room, for instance, is one hundred and forty-three feet long and fifty-one feet wide. In it there is a silver throne. There is not a finer palace in Europe."

ROYAL PALACE, STOCKHOLM.

In our opinion the club was justified in the general expression of admiration which followed this description. Henry mentally resolved that when he went traveling he would be sure and see this palace.

"You can at once see," continued Uncle George, "when you consider the immense number of islands, that the little excursions which can be made from Stockholm by steamer to the charming little resorts around are simply innumerable. There is one park called the Djurgard, which can be reached in a few minutes' ride by steamer, that is certainly magnificent. It is twenty

miles in circumference, and is beautifully laid out. There are hills and valleys, and finely kept roads winding around among great forest trees. Here is
a view of it. Rosendale Castle is one of the buildings of the park. On another lovely island, but a few minutes' ride, is the Royal Summer Palace of Drott-ningholm. It is surrounded by beautifully kept grounds, and contains quantities of curiosities and works of art.

"You that have read history know that Sweden has at two different times exercised consid-erable influence in Europe within recent centu-ries, and conse-quently there are statues and many memen-toes of their two great war-rior kings—Charles XII. and Gustavus Adolphus. I presume that most of you have heard of Gustavus Adol-phus; if not, you will when you read general his-history. He was a great general, and made Sweden

PALACE.

ROSENDALE CASTLE.

KNIGHTS' HOUSE.

everywhere respected. During what is known as the Thirty Years' War Gus-tavus Adolphus was the great general on the Protestant side. He was about the only one who could cope with the great imperial commanders, Tilly and

CARRYING THE BODY OF CHARLES XII TO STOCKHOLM

Wallenstein. He was killed at the moment of victory. You need not be surprised to hear that the uniform in which he was killed, all stained with blood, is still preserved in one of the museums of Stockholm. We have here a view of a large bronze statue of Gustavus Adolphus.

STATUE OF GUSTAVUS ADOLPHUS.

"Another of their great soldier kings was Charles XII. At the early age of fifteen he took up arms in defense of Sweden. Wonderful success followed his efforts, but he suffered a terrible defeat at the hands of Peter the Great. He was finally killed in attempting to conquer Norway, though it is thought by some that he was assassinated by one of his own soldiers. This large picture shows us the funeral cortege conveying his body to Stockholm. He was indeed a strange character, and, though a great general, his reign was on the whole disastrous to Sweden."

After the club had examined these pictures, and a few questions had been asked and answered in regard to Stockholm, Mr. Adams continued:

"Now, I want to talk to you generally about Scandinavia. You know it is perfectly natural for every people to think their country and their people to be a little better than any other country or people. The Scandinavians are especially noted in this particular. They do love to dwell on their past greatness, and they can see a great many more beauties in their country than any

traveler can. Of course, the larger part of Norway and Sweden is very picturesque as far as scenery is concerned. Here is a view of Norwegian scenery—
Lake Bandak. You must notice the imposing mountains coming right down
to the shore. This is quite a pleasure resort, and little excursions are made
from Christiana by tourists. The section of country in which this lake is

LAKE BANDAK.

situated is Thelemarken, in the southern part of Norway. It is one of the
most picturesque provinces. It has a number of lakes, fine water-falls, and a
variety of mountain scenery; but it is so rugged that there are few good
roads, and in consequence, if you want to study Norwegian character, there
is a good place. Here is a little account of the Norwegians which Ida may
read for us. This is about the only way we can get Ida to let us know she

is here," added Uncle George with a smile, as he handed her the book. Ida took just as much interest as the rest, but she was naturally very quiet.

She read as follows: " In no land is hospitality more open-handed and unaffected than in Norway; and though these features are naturally becoming

COSTUMES OF THELEMARKEN.

blunted along the beaten lines of travel, the genuine goodness of heart, fine gentlemanly feeling, and entire absence of that sordidness which is, so often seen even in primitive regions, cannot fail to strike the unprejudiced observer. One of the peculiarities of the Norwegian farmer is, that when visiting a friend he must ignore all the preparations made for his entertainment. He will see the coffee roasted and the cups set out, and then, just when the good wife is about to offer him her hospitality, he gets up, bids the family good-bye, and is only persuaded to remain after some resistance. Every cup must be filled to overflowing, otherwise the host would be thought stingy. When milk, brandy, or beer is offered, the guest invariably begs it will not be wasted on him, and then, after emptying the cup, declares that it is too much —going through the same formality, it may be, three or four times."

After the laugh had subsided Uncle George told them that every people had their peculiar ideas as to what was appropriate, which would often strike others as very absurd, and then he called their attention to a picture representing the costumes of the inhabitants of Thelemarken.

"Talking about national customs, there is one Swedish custom commemorated at Christmas Eve that pleases all who observe it. Each house raises a sheaf of grain to the roof, so that the wild birds may have their Christmas, too. Here we have a view of such a scene, and you notice the boys coasting. Boys generally manage to have a pretty good time wherever they may happen to be.

"Now I am going to show you some views that will acquaint us with another feature of Scandinavian life. You all know that Norway and Sweden extend quite a ways north. The northern part of the peninsula, in fact, lies beyond the Arctic Circle, and so is in the—well, Henry, can you tell us what zone?"

"Why, yes—North Frigid Zone," answered Henry, with quite a complacent air of wisdom.

"That's it," said Uncle George, "and so, of course, the winters are very long, cold, and dreary; the summers short, hot, and the days very long—in fact, at the extreme north it is practically day all the time for several weeks. The sun only disappears below the horizon for a short while, and you, of course, know that in some places you can see the sun all night long."

"Why, how funny! Did you see that, uncle?" broke in Henry.

"Well, no," said Uncle George. "I never happened to be in the extreme north of Norway in the summer time, but I have talked with a number who have been there. But what I was going to talk about was the people who live in those northern regions. Does any one know who they are?"

"Ain't they the Lapps?" said Nettic.

"And the Finns?" added Burt.

CHRISTMAS CUSTOM   THE KALKE

SWEDISH WINTER CUSTOMS.

"That is right. Now it may not be generally known that these people, the Lapps and Finns, are only a fragment of the people that once extended very generally over Europe, but now they are to be found in the extreme north of Europe. Here we have a view of Lapland. It looks pretty dreary, don't it? The Lapps are a nomadic people."

LAPPS.

"What kind of people, uncle?" said Henry.

"Nomadic, Henry—that is, wandering, having no fixed place of living, though this is not true of them in all places. If you were to see them, you would probably notice their round face, short flat nose, and wide mouth. They are named according to their manner of gaining a livelihood. There are the sea Lapps, who live by fishing along the shores of the sea; the river Lapps along the river; and the mountain Lapps. The reindeer, as you know, is the animal that is of the greatest service to the Lapps. They keep them as we do cattle. It is their sole wealth. It gives the milk and butter, and it is their beast of burden. Its skin supplies them with clothing, and when old or infirm its flesh is used as food. It feeds on lichens, mosses, willows, and

the dwarf Arctic vegetation in general.   In winter it digs under the snow for
its food, which consists almost entirely of reindeer moss.   Here is a nearer
view of a herd of reindeer."

" What would they do without it?" exclaimed Henry.

REINDEER.

" Well, there is no animal that would quite take its place, that is sure,"
added Uncle George.   " I only want to add that once on a time the reindeer
lived over Europe generally.   In what is now Southern France they once on
a time were very abundant, and it is equally sure that at that time the climate
must have been very different from what it is now.

" The remainder of the evening we will devote to Russia.   This is a very
interesting, but also a very difficult, country to visit.   It will be necessary for
us to have our passports correct in every respect, or we won't get in, in the
first place ; and, in traveling around, it will be very necessary to keep them
properly *viseed*, or we will be getting in trouble all the time."

" What is a passport, and why didn't you tell us about it before?" asked
Nettie.

" I have not mentioned them because we have not needed them heretofore. A passport is a document given by the authorized officer of a state. It is supposed to give the holder the support and protection of his government, and entitles him to the protection of the government in whose territory he

NICOLAI BRIDGE.

may be traveling. We will suppose that everything is all straight with us, and so we will go directly to St. Petersburg. Show them where it is, Burt."

Burt pointed it out, and the club saw that it was almost directly east of Stockholm, at the further end of the Gulf of Finland, at the mouth of the River Neva.

" Here," resumed Mr. Adams, " is our first view of St. Petersburg. You

6

see the Neva River, and the one stone bridge crossing it. The Neva is not a very long river, but it is wide, and it brings down an enormous quantity of clear, cold, blue water to the Gulf of Finland.

"In the beginning of the eighteenth century this territory belonged to Sweden, but Peter the Great annexed it, and determined to build a new

STATUE OF PETER THE GREAT.

capital at this place, which was simply one big marsh. So he set a whole army of men at work deepening the river, raising the islands, driving whole forests of piles into the swampy ground for a foundation. Year after year this work went forward. Foreign workmen were hired to embellish the city. Rich Russian nobles and merchants were commanded to come there and erect buildings. Here we have an equestrian statue of this great Czar. Notice the enormous bowlder on which the statue rests. It weighs about fifteen hundred tons. It was found about four miles away in a swamp, and took five hundred men and a large number of horses about five weeks to move it to its present resting place.

"Peter the Great was the founder of modern Russia. He was a strange character. When he commenced his reign his people were only about half civilized. When he was building his new capital he lived in a little cottage

THE WINTER PALACE.

on the banks of the Neva. That building is still preserved with the greatest care. Contrasted with the poor, almost insignificant, little cottage inhabited by Peter, the palace of the present Czar is a very great change. I have a view of it here. It is the famous Winter Palace. The first time it was built it occupied over thirty years in building, but it was destroyed by fire fifty years ago, and the Czar then on the throne had it rebuilt in a single year. A great army of workmen were employed, and the whole resources of Russia were brought to bear on it. Now, Ida, you read about this palace."

Ida took the book that Uncle George handed, and read the following extract:

"The interior of the palace is a marvel of splendor; oriental luxury and occidental splendor are both apparent everywhere. Curtains and tapestries of silk, satin, and damask; vast mirrors, ornaments of amber, lapis-lazuli, marble and malachite statues, paintings, and bronzes are all mingled in unimaginable profusion. In the throne room is an image of St. George; before it burns continually a lamp of massive gold, suspended by chains of precious stones. The numerous splendid rooms are crowded with historic and other paintings. The drawing-room of the empress has gilded walls and ceilings. In one room are deposited the crown jewels. Here on the imperial scepter of Russia gleams the great Orloff diamond, said to have once formed the eye of an Indian idol. It is valued at nearly two million dollars."

"Uncle, I wanted to ask," said Henry as Ida stopped reading, "what is that oriental and that other kind of luxury Ida read about?"

"You mean oriental and occidental luxury," said Uncle George. "Well, oriental means the east or eastern countries, and occidental the western countries; or, in other words, here was a mixture of the grandeur of both Asia and Europe. Does that make it clear?"

"Oh, yes; I guess I understand now," replied Henry.

"It was Peter who defeated Charles XII. of Sweden that we were talking about a little while ago, and I see that we have here a picture from a painting representing Peter on that famous battle field."

"By the way," continued Uncle George, "the palace stands near the Neva. On the opposite shore is an immense castle. Now the Neva, as you might guess, freezes over in the winter, and sometimes remains frozen until late in the spring. While in this state, of course, foreign vessels cannot approach the city. So you can see how glad they all are when the ice finally breaks up. When that event happens, whether by day or night, the big guns in the castle are fired, and the commandant of the castle is rowed across to the palace and presents a goblet of clear cold water, dipped from the middle of the stream, to the Czar. After sipping some of the water, the Czar returns the goblet filled with silver coins."

"I should think the soldiers would be sure to get a good big goblet if they get it back filled with money," said Willie.

"They do say," replied Uncle George, with a smile, "that the tendency

PETER THE GREAT ON THE BATTLE-FIELD OF PULTOVA.   93

was for the cup to increase in size, but they finally compromised the matter by agreeing on a fixed sum to be given by the Czar."

"I see I have here," he continued, turning the pages of his album, "pictures of two quite noted rulers of Russia. Catherine II. was one of the most remarkable women of the eighteenth century. She made her way to the throne by deposing and murdering her husband; and she was a very despotic and arbitrary ruler. But, for all that, her reign was a remarkably brilliant one for Russia.

CATHERINE II.

Nicholas I. is another singular character in the later history of Russia. He was known as the Iron Czar. He was the autocrat of Europe. But he was behind the times in many ways. By the way, he was the one that built that famous Winter Palace that we looked at a moment ago."

"He wasn't the Czar that was killed a few years ago, was he?" asked Willie.

NICHOLAS I.

"No, that was his son, Alexander II.; but I presume we have had enough of history, and so we will turn to our pictures again."

"Here is a view of the Cathedral of St. Isaac. That is the finest cathedral in all Russia. The top of the cross you see on the dome is three hundred and sixty-six feet from the ground. To get a suitable foundation a vast number of piles, twenty-one feet in length, were driven into the ground. It cost a million dollars just for that part of it. The central cupola you see is covered with copper, overlaid with gold, and from the little rotunda above

CATHEDRAL OF ST. ISAAC.

it a grand view is obtained of the city. As you might suppose, the interior is magnificent. Porphyry, jasper, malachite, and other costly materials are freely used. The inner sanctuary, into which no woman is allowed to enter, is approached by a bronze door, having on each side a column of lapis lazuli costing thirty thousand dollars apiece."

"Why can't a woman go into the inner sanctuary?" said Nettie, in a rather defiant tone.

"I cannot answer that question," said Uncle George. "Probably for some religious reasons," he added.

"The religion is Catholic, I suppose," said Burt.

"No, you are mistaken there, unless you make an explanation. You see there are two great divisions of the Catholic Church—the Roman Catho-

METROPOLITAN OF ST. PETERSBURG.

lic and the Greek Catholic. I have here a picture representing the Metropolitan of St. Petersburg and his clergy.

"But we must hurry along. I will now show you some views in Moscow: point it out on the map, Burt—southeast of St. Petersburg, distance about four hundred miles. You must notice the railroad, how straight it is. When the engineers laid before the Czar (the same Nicholas we were just talking about) plans for that road, it zigzagged and curved, as railroads generally do, to avoid obstacles and strike important towns; but he took a ruler and drew a straight line between the two cities, and said 'Build it that way.' And that is the way it was built.

MOSCOW.

"Here is a general view of the city, and in many respects this is the most interesting city in Russia. It was the old capital before St. Petersburg was built, and every Czar must go to Moscow to be crowned. This is not a very old place as age is reckoned in Europe, being only about seven centuries old.

"Moscow is full of interesting places and mementoes. In this picture we have what is known as the great bell of Moscow, and in the background the most famous cathedral that stands in the Kremlin, or citadel of Moscow. I might remark that, in the Greek Church, bells play a very important part in the ceremony; and so every cathedral is plentifully supplied with them. This big bell is so very big that it is unmanageable. It weighs nearly two hundred tons."

THE GREAT BELL AT MOSCOW.

"There is a piece chipped out of the side," said Willie.

"Yes? Well, that piece, Willie, weighs about eleven tons," said Uncle George, "so there is no danger of any one's taking it off."

"What about the cathedral?" asked Burt.

"Yes, I was going to say that that is the Cathedral of the Assumption, or Repose of the Virgin. It is not a very large cathedral, but all the primates of Moscow are elected within its walls,.and it is very rich. There is one picture in it of the Virgin, which the orthodox Russians are supposed to believe was painted by St. Luke. The picture is fairly covered with jewels. I have seen their value estimated at more than a quarter of a million dollars. .But the greatest importance of this cathedral is, that all the Czars of Russia, from the days of Ivan the Terrible, have been crowned in it.   In this cere-mony no one but the Czar takes part.   You see he is the head of both church and state.   Alone he kneels before the assembled multitude in prayer; then he places the crown upon his own head."

"Who was that terrible Czar you spoke of?" asked Nettie.

"Ivan the Terrible?   He was a sixteenth century Czar, and was one of those strange characters that now and then flit across the stage of history.   In

ENTRY OF IVAN INTO KAZAN.

some respects he was undoubtedly a madman, and gave way at times to the most fiendish cruelties.   Yet he accomplished a great deal for Russia, and materially advanced her in civilization.   Here we have a picture of this famous Czar after his conquest of Kazan, a large district in the eastern part of Russia.

"Moscow might be called the 'City of Churches,' and we might remark that the Russians are very religious in a certain sense.   There is scarcely a bridge or a street corner without its shrine—some rudely pictured saint with a burning taper before it. Every passer-by bows and worships. The rich, riding by in their carriage, rise up in reverential silence; and the poorest

CATHEDRAL OF ST. BASIL.

street beggar does not forget to uncover and spend a moment in prayer. But religion sits rather loosely. Here is a picture of another great famous

cathedral, built by that same Ivan I was just telling you about to commemorate his great victory in Kazan. Hundreds of artists were kidnapped
from Lubeck to assist in the adornment of the building. It is said that when
the building was completed Ivan had the architect's eyes put out, to prevent
him from erecting anything equal to it."

"I shouldn't think he would dare to do that," exclaimed Nettie.

"The Czars of Russia apparently care very little for the rights or
wrongs of their subjects. It is the most despotic country in Europe."

"Wasn't Moscow burned once?" inquired Willie.

"Yes, and that makes me think—have any of you ever heard about
Napoleon's march to Moscow?"

"Yes," said some. But as Henry wanted to hear about it, Uncle George
told him how proudly the French army entered Moscow as conquerors, but
the second night after their entry the city was fired in hundreds of places;
and as the fire engines had been removed, nothing could check the flames.
As a consequence, almost the entire city was destroyed. Palaces and temples,
works of art and luxury, buildings which had stood for many years, all were
destroyed. And so the French army was compelled to retreat just as winter
was setting in. Then the Russian forces appeared on the scene, and as a
result of their attacks, and the exposure to the weather and of hunger—for
no food could be obtained—only a small portion of the French army reached
France in safety. From that disastrous expedition dates the downfall of
Napoleon."

"Who was Czar at that time?" inquired Burt.

"Alexander I., father of Nicholas I., whose picture we looked at a
moment ago, and great-grandfather of the present Czar. But now let us
return to our views. We have been talking so much about churches that we
will now look at a pleasure resort. The principal one is the Petrofski
Gardens. This is a great resort in summer time. The road leading to it is
thronged with vehicles and well-dressed pedestrians, who go there to enjoy
the music and flowers. Guards and police keep order at the gates. Within
there are varied attractions—promenades and lawns, artificial caves, glens
and grottoes. In the evening, avenues of many colored lights and festooned
arches conduct to pagodas used as theatres, and there are, in addition, grand
displays of fireworks."

"That looks awful cold," said Henry, referring to the picture.

CHATEAU OF PETROFSKI.

"Yes; that is the winter scene, Of course, this gay season only lasts a few months."

"What is that very nice looking house with so many cupolas?" asked Nettie.

"That is the chateau built by the Empress Elizabeth. Napoleon stopped there for a few days after the burning of Moscow. Now I think the balance of the evening we had better talk about the Russian people generally. Burt, can you tell me the racial name of the Russians?"

"I don't know what it is, unless it is Slavonians."

"That is right, and I am glad you recalled it. All the European people are called Aryans, but there are great divisions of them, such as the Teutons,

SAMOYEDE ENCAMPMENT.

Scandinavians, and Slavonians. The Slavonians constitute the people of Russia and several smaller bodies of people in Southeastern Europe, such as the Servians, Montenegrins, and others. Russia, as you know, is an immense large country—not only in Europe, but in Asia. So, of course, there has been a wonderful mixture of people. But, as a whole, the people are Slavs. Way up in the northern part of Russia we come upon a people much like the Lapps and Finns; and, for that matter, one large district of Russia is called Finland, since it is inhabited almost exclusively by Finns. But the special people I have in mind are the Samoyedes, and here is a picture of one of their encampments."

"And there are some more reindeers, ain't there, uncle?" said Henry.

"Yes. The reindeer is found generally in the extreme northern part of Europe and Asia, and these people would be just as much at a loss to know what to do without these useful animals as the Lapps. But now, returning to the Russians proper, we must say that the Slavs are much more united than any other Aryan people. You see, they are virtually all under one government. The other little kingdoms, like Servia, are insignificant in themselves; and then, besides, they are all under Russian influence, and it may be that before many years they, too, will be a part of Russia. Then, again, they are all united in religion—they are Greek Catholics. There are other religious sects, to be sure, but they are only a small fraction of the whole. Then, besides, they have similar customs. I am a little afraid you will not feel much interested in this matter, but I want to tell you a little about their village life."

There was a general desire to hear, and so Uncle George continued:

"You remember the other night we talked a little about tribal society and about the clans."

"Oh, I know; up in Scotland," said Henry.

"Just so. Well, the Slavonian people generally show very distinct traces of such a life. They are not called clans, but *mirs*. Properly speaking, each village in Russia is a mir, and governs itself and owns its own land, and all in the mir stand on an equality. They are supposed to divide the land among their members every three years. They execute their own laws, and can banish a refractory member to Siberia if they want to. In process of time the chiefs of these mirs became an hereditary class, and the common mass of the people became literally slaves, but they always clung to their old organization. A few years ago these slaves, or serfs, as they were called, were freed by the Czar; but unfortunately, owing to the workings of a great many causes, their condition is not much better. In a great many respects Russia is as yet an undeveloped country, just as they have retained traces of their old tribal life, after the rest of Europe have forgotten it. They are backward in other respects, and so they have a great deal of experience to go through with that the other nations of Europe have passed through.

7

"Their government, which is now the most absolute in all Europe, will have to be brought in some way to the constitutional basis. And the great mass of the people have yet to be educated, and throw off that old dependence on tribal customs which now hinders them. In short, Russia is now going through a very critical time in its history. There is a widespread discontent among the masses of the people at the existing order of things. And some

VILLAGE FÊTE IN RUSSIA.

day there is going to be a wonderful upheaval, which will shake Europe to its center.

"What about the Nihilists, uncle?" asked Burt. "I have read a good deal about them lately—are they good or bad people?" he added.

"I presume," replied Uncle George, "that we have all been prejudiced against Nihilists because we did not understand the true state of affairs in

Russia. The Nihilists, Henry" (noting the inquiring look on his face), "are a secret body of people having for their object the overthrow of existing laws and customs in Russia. We have been apt to think of them as Anarchists, who wanted to overthrow all laws, and have naturally supposed they included only the worst elements of the population. But Mr. Keenan, who has been writing and lecturing about them, tells us that they include in their ranks some of the very best people in Russia.

RUSSIAN VILLAGE.

"But we must not take up too much of the time with such talk as this," continued Uncle George. "As I said before, the great feature of Russian life is villages. There are comparatively few large towns and cities, and we would think a Russian village a very dull place to live in. Here we have a view of a village in Southern Russia. In a Russian village there are sure to be several crosses often elaborately carved and covered with deeply cut inscriptions, or decorated with gay colors. The houses are nearly always built with the gable end to the street, and in the center of the gable there is usually a window opening on a balcony."

"How do you travel around there? I don't see many railroads," asked Willie.

RUSSIAN TARANTASS.

"In districts off of the railroads you will have to rely on the posting system. That is to say, there are official post-houses where horses, drivers, and conveyances are furnished. But I can assure you that you will not relish this sort of traveling. The accommodations are wretched. The carriages, or wagons, have no springs, and the horses are driven on the keen run. Riding in an old lumber wagon is luxury compared with it.

"Of course, you understand that I have been talking about the peasantry, which includes the great bulk of the people of Russia. There is, of

course, another class, including the rich and well-to-do people, and the
nobility. I have here a view of the costumes of ladies of this class. These
are from various towns. As you may suppose, the dress of the peasantry is
in keeping with what they eat. A cotton shirt, a pair of linen trousers, and

RUSSIAN WOMEN.

bark shoes in summer suffices; sheep-skin clothing in winter, and coarse
woolens. So, you see, you observe all kinds of life in Russia.

"Now we will devote just a few minutes to Siberia. You, of course,
know that Russia in Europe is only a small part of the Russian Empire.
We have been accustomed to think of Siberia as a most desolate region. But
our enterprising American traveler, Mr. Keenau, has recently published a

wonderfully interesting series of articles, and we are probably all surprised
to find how much of that country is really fertile land, and what a bright
future is ahead of it.   I have here a view of Lake Baikal in Siberia.   This
lake is nearly four hundred miles long, but not more than twenty or twenty-
five miles wide.   Its basin is quite elevated, as it is more than twelve hundred
feet above the level of the sea.

LAKE BAIKAL.

"Siberia, as you know, is mainly distinguished as the place where Russia
sends her prisoners.   It is their great penal colony.   You might think it
would be easy to get away from such a large country, but it is extremely
difficult to do so.   To the north there is a frozen ocean ; to the south there
are almost impassable mountains, dreary deserts, and the most inhospitable
part of Asia.   Probably in no other way does the terrible short-coming of the

Russian Government show itself more plainly than in their treatment of the exiles to Siberia. When we read Mr. Keenan's articles on this subject, it is impossible to repress the feeling of indignation. We feel almost as if the whole civilized world ought to interfere. It is impossible to escape the conclusion that such a system cannot last. We feel sure that the storm must arise that will deluge all Russia in blood. The sorrowful feature is that such a conflict must cause a vast amount of innocent suffering.

"Now we have gone far enough for this evening. I think we are getting along real well, and next time we will take in Teutonic Europe—that is, Holland, Belgium, Germany, and Austria. But let me ask you: Are you satisfied? Is it what you expected? Perhaps you are tired, and don't much care to keep it up."

There was a very general expression of approval. Even quiet Ida expressed herself as having a splendid time. As for Henry, though he had taken possession of a sofa near his mother and Aunt Mary, and there was a very tired and sleepy look on his chubby face, he said: "Why, of course, we want to go on; we have only just got started."

PETER THE GREAT.

CHAPTER IV.

TEUTONIC EUROPE.

NOVELTY had, of course, worn off at the third meeting of the club, but the substantial results remained. Many little details of history and geography had a new meaning. At school, Henry's teacher was astonished, when she asked him some question about St. Petersburg, to find how much he knew about the place. It was indeed a great improvement; for, to tell the truth, Henry was one of those bright little fellows who, full of life and energy, had not yet realized the necessity of study, and did not know how to apply himself. The winter had been mild and pleasant for that locality, and, as a consequence, there had not been much sleighing or skating to occupy the time of the young folks. This, perhaps, was one reason why they looked forward with interest to the meetings of the club. Children will be children after all, and their little hearts and hands will as naturally turn to what promises them a good time as flowers turn their opening buds to the sunshine.

Uncle George found himself thinking considerably about the next tour, arranging his pictures in order, and getting up his part of the programme. Mrs. Scott had fully intended to accompany the children once more; but just at the last moment something detained her, and so the children went alone, though the coachman drove for them. As usual, everything was in readiness, and Uncle George soon called them to order around the library table, on which he had previously placed a number of books, including the indispensable atlas.

"This evening," he began, "we are going to visit Teutonic Europe. In our last trip, you remember, we visited Slavonic Europe and Scandinavia. Now, the Scandinavians are very closely related to the Teutons. The English, the Scandinavians, and the Teutons form the Germanic people of Europe. The first country we will stop at will be Holland."

At a sign from Uncle George, Burt had opened the large atlas at the map of Holland so that all could see it.

"You have all heard of the dykes of Holland. Here is a picture of a small part of the coast protected by a dyke."

DYKES ON COAST OF HOLLAND.

"It looks like a railroad, don't it, uncle? And what is it there for?" said Henry.

"A large part of Holland, Henry, is below the level of the sea. In fact, a large part of Holland is artificial land; so, to keep the waters off of the land, they have had to build a great big dam along the coast. We have little idea of what a tremendous amount of work and cost all this has involved. Why in Zealand alone, which is only one of the provinces of Holland, there are nearly two hundred and sixty miles of dykes. The province of Friesland is defended for fifty-five miles by three rows of dykes of a very expensive kind. Every great city in Holland is protected by dykes."

"I should think they wouldn't want to live there," said Nettie.

"On the contrary, the Dutch are very proud and very fond of their little country. They take a great deal of pride in the fact that they have changed a country consisting of swamp and marsh, or shifting sand, into one of the most fertile countries of Europe. And they have a great deal to be proud of

QUAY IN AMSTERDAM.

in their history. That little neck of land dared to defy Spain when Spain was the most formidable power in Europe, and it came out victorious in the fight, too. And there was a time once when Holland led the world in commerce and voyages of discovery. But we must hurry on.

"To give you an idea of a Dutch city and its scenery, we will go at once to Amsterdam. Here we have a view of Amsterdam. You know at St. Peters-

VIEWS IN AMSTERDAM.

burg we talked about the numerous piles that had to be driven for a foundation. Almost every town in Holland rests on piles. This would strike you
as a very queer place. You see the River Amsel empties into the Y, a branch
of Zuyder Zee, at this place. There are about ninety islands, and a great
many canals ; and on these canals are a great many ships, coming and going.
Here is a little extract for our reader," saying which he handed Ida a book.

Ida read as follows : "At every turn of a street you see in a new direction
three, four, or even six draw-bridges, some rising, some falling, some closed,
and some in motion, presenting a confused perspective of beams and chains,
as if Amsterdam were composed of so many enemies' quarters, all fortified
against each other. Canals as broad as rivers form here and there spacious
basins, around which you can go by a succession of bridges joined one to the
other. From every crossing can be seen distant perspectives of other bridges,
canals, shipping, edifices, all veiled in a light mist, which makes them look
more distant. The canals are covered with ships and barges ; and in the
streets that flank them are seen on one side heaps of casks, bales, and sacks ;
on the other a row of splendid shops. Here a draw-bridge rises to give
passage to a ship; there the people swarm upon one which has but just fallen
into its place again ; further on a raft ferries over a group of persons from
the other side of the canal; from the bottom of the street a steamboat is just
setting off; at the opposite extremity a long file of laden barges are just
coming in."

"How large is Amsterdam ?" inquired Willie.

"Nearly three hundred and twenty thousand," replied Uncle George.
"I have here," he continued, "a collection of views in this city. You must
notice the canals right in the very heart of the city. Holland is cut up by
numerous canals. Very often the canals are higher than the surrounding
land, and then the water off of the land is pumped into the canal. For this
purpose wind-mills are used. These wind-mills are one of the sights of
Holland. You see, they have no water power, there is no coal, and so the
people have to fall back on the wind. You can hardly look out of doors
anywhere in the country without seeing a wind-mill. They do everything—
drain the land, grind the grain, break up stone to be made into cement. A
person's wealth and social position is estimated by the number of wind-mills
he has.

"Did you know that the Dutch cities and villages were celebrated for their cleanliness? They are excessively neat about the house. Everything is frequently scrubbed and scoured; but every traveler will say that the Dutch nose is not easily disturbed. There is not much current to the canals, and sometimes they smell anything but sweet. But not very far from the city is the famous village of Broek, said to be the cleanest town in the world. It used to be forbidden to smoke in the street without a cover on the pipe, for fear you would scatter the ashes. If a citizen sees a leaf or straw fall upon the pavement, he is expected to come out and pick it up, and throw it in the canal. Here is a little description of a dairy farm near Broek which Ida may read for us."

Opening the book, Ida read the following: " Many people among us who wear expensive clothes and sport gold watches have not such pretty and clean houses as those in which the cows of Broek reside. Before entering, you are requested to wipe your feet on a mat laid there for that purpose. The pavement of the stalls is of various colored bricks, so clean that the hand could be passed over it; the walls are covered with pine wood; the windows decorated with muslin curtains and pots of flowers; the mangers are painted; the animals themselves are scraped, combed, washed, and, that they may not soil their coats, their tails are held up by a cord which is attached to a nail in the ceiling." (Here the reading was interrupted by Henry. He could keep his face straight no longer.) "A clear stream of water running through between the stalls carries of all impurities, except under the animals' feet. There is not a straw or a stain to be seen; and the air is so pure that if you close your eyes, you may imagine yourself in a drawing-room."

" I think you will agree with me," said Uncle George, as Ida closed the book and the laugh subsided, " that Broek deserves its name. It is said that the Dutch clean everything they possess once every day, and three times on Saturday. There is, of course, a little good-natured exaggeration in this account. But the butter and cheese of Holland are famous everywhere. Enormous quantities of cheese are exported to London every year; and even farther than that, for the celebrated Edam cheese that we buy in this country is imported from Holland.

"About ten miles to the west of Amsterdam is an interesting old town— Haarlem. When you enter the city, you see on every side canals, windmills, draw-bridges, and fishing boats. Near the center of the city is a large square, a portion of which is shown in this cut. The quaint old town hall is on one side of the square. By the way, Haarlem is noted for its flowers. About the end of April the country is ablaze with flowers. Great quantities of them are sent even as far as London. Tulips are their especial favorite. By the way, once on a time there was a wonderful craze over these flowers in Holland. Fabulous sums of money were paid for rare specimens. I have read of ten thousand dollars being offered and refused for one bulb of an unusual variety. But the craze spent itself finally."

"How foolish to give so much money as that just for a flower!" exclaimed Ida.

TOWN HALL, HAARLEM.

But Uncle George said that they were no more foolish in this matter than people generally are when they go wild over speculation.

"Now, to show you how the Dutch go to work to increase the area of their land, I will speak of Haarlem Lake, or sea, which used to extend between Haarlem and Amsterdam, separated by a very narrow stretch of land from the Y. Now that lake covered over forty-five thousand acres of land, and we need not wonder that the Dutch wanted to get rid of it. So they

threw a great big double dyke around it, inclosing a canal; put four mon-
strous steam pumps at work pumping the water out of the lake into the
canal.   In four years' time the job was completed, the lake was no more.
You can imagine, though, with how much care the dyke keeping out the
water of the Y is looked after.   If that should break, thousands of people
would be drowned, and many millions of dollars worth of property destroyed.

"Uncle," said Burt, "what is the difference between the Dutch and the
Germans?   I know there is some difference," he added.

THE BOOMPJES, ROTTERDAM.

"The difference is about the same as that between the Scotch and the English.   The people of
Prussia are properly Germans, and they feel insulted
to be called Dutch.   But we must hurry on.

"Another Dutch city of some importance is Rotterdam, right in the
southwestern part of Holland, where the River Meuse begins to open out to
the sea.   This city has a big future before it, and probably at no very distant
day will be the commercial capital of Holland.   Along the bank of the Meuse
a dyke is built called the Boompjes.   This is the busiest part of the city.   I
have here an interesting account of a traveler's impression of Rotterdam,
including his visit to this dyke, which Willie may read this time."

Rather confused, since he did not expect to read, Willie took the book which Uncle George had opened, and read: "From canal to canal, and from bridge to bridge, I finally reached the dyke of the Boompjez upon the Meuse, where boils and bubbles all the life of the great commercial city. On the left extends a long row of small many-colored steamboats, which start every hour of the day for Dordrecht, Arnheim, Gonda, Schiedam, Brilla, and Zealand, and continually send forth clouds of white smoke and the sound of their cheerful bells. To the right lie the large ships which make the voyage to various European ports, mingled with fine three-masted vessels bound for the East Indies, with names written in golden letters—Java, Sumatra, Borneo, Samarang—carrying the fancy to those distant and savage countries like the echoes of distant voices. In front the Meuse covered with boats and barks, and the distant shore with a forest of beech trees, wind-mills, and towers; and over all the unique sky full of gleams of light, and gloomy clouds fleeting and changing in their movement, as if repeating the restless labor on the earth below."

ERASMUS

"One little item of interest," continued Uncle George as Willie ceased reading, "ought to be known. In the public square of this city stands a statue to Erasmus. I don't know as you have heard much about him, but when you read history about the general revival of learning, which led to the Reformation, you will find that Erasmus played quite a conspicuous part in this work. He was born in Rotterdam."

"Oh, I read somewhere," exclaimed Burt, "about the Reformation, that Erasmus laid the egg, and Luther hatched it. What did they mean?"

"They meant that Erasmus by his writings really laid the foundation for the Reformation, which Luther carried out. But, coming back to Rotterdam, you must understand that the whole of the city is intersected by canals, broad, long, and deep, capable of accommodating vessels of heavy tonnage. It is interesting to walk through a Dutch city and find everywhere

these canals, with streets on either side, and trees along the side of almost
every street, and you can never get away from the ships. Right in the very
heart of the city you will find the large ships discharging their cargoes.

CHURCH OF ST. LAWRENCE.

You see the masts of ships among the houses, above the trees, beside the
churches, and all along the houses. Here is a picture which gives you an
idea of what it is like. The church, I might remark, is the Church of
St. Lawrence, and from the tall spire we get a splendid view of the city.

"Not far from Rotterdam is the town of Deft, from the harbor of which place, called Delf Haven, the *Mayflower* sailed with the Puritans when they left Holland for this country, so every American should remember that place. But it is also memorable to the historian as the place of the assassination of William the Silent. The picture I have here is not that celebrated Prince,

WILLIAM, PRINCE OF ORANGE.

but William of Orange, who afterwards became King William III. of England. His great ancestor, William the Silent, was a most remarkable man. I think every one that reads an account of his life must admire him. He it was who conducted the ever-memorable defense of Holland against Spain. He was indeed the father of his people. He went through life, ' bearing the load of a people's sorrow upon his shoulders, with a smiling face. As long as he
8

lived, he was the guiding star of a whole brave nation; and when he died, the
little children cried in the streets.' This beautiful monument stands in the

MAUSOLEUM OF WILLIAM THE SILENT.

old church of Deft. It may be described as a sort of small temple in black
and white marble, loaded with ornaments, and sustained by columns, between
which are four statues representing Liberty, Prudence, Justice, and Religion.

"This old church in Deft is almost a sacred spot for the Hollanders. There is buried their great admiral, Van Tromp. After one of his victories over the English he sailed up and down the English Channel, with a broom at his mast-head, as much as to say that he could sweep the English off the sea if he wished.

DORDRECHT.

"But we must hurry on. I will only call your attention to one more Dutch town, and here is a view of Dordrecht, or Dort, about ten miles from Rotterdam. It gives us a good idea of a Holland city, with a canal right through the heart of the city.

Now I want to talk a while about the Zuyder Zee and the cities along the shore. Burt, you point out the Zuyder Zee so that all can see it. You can all see what a large part of Holland it covers. It was not in existence before the thirteenth century. But during that century the sea gradually overflowed the land. When Holland was at the height of her prosperity, there were numerous cities all along the shores which were extremely prosperous. There is Hoorn, once a most prosperous city; it was a ship sailing from that city that discovered and named Cape Horn. Of course, you all know where that is. Then there is the town of Enkhuizen, now an insignificant place; yet less than two centuries ago it had a population of over forty thousand. On the opposite side there is Stavoren; now it is an insignificant village with perhaps five hundred inhabitants, with crumbling houses. Yet there was a time once when this city was one of the leaders in the Hanseatic League we talked about the other night, and was so powerful that she forced treaties from Sweden and Scotland giving her sailors extra privileges."

"What is the matter with all those places," asked Burt; "when they got a good start, why did not they keep it?"

"One reason is that the Zuyder Zee is filling up. It is almost unnavigable. Where there were once fine harbors are now great sandbanks. And so we need not wonder that the Dutch government proposes to drain the Zuyder Zee."

"The way they did that other lake by Haarlem?" asked Henry.

"Yes, mainly so. They propose to build an enormous dyke from Medemblik to Stavoren—right at the narrowest part you see—and pump it out. Then they will have to make canals to the towns along its shore. That will give Holland nearly a thousand square miles of fertile land. There are a few little islands in the Zuyder Zee that are very interesting to the traveler. Such is the Island of Marken. It is so retired from the world that few strangers ever go there; still the people are happy and contented."

"I should think they would be awful lonesome and would want to get away," said Henry.

"On the contrary, they think there is no place like their little specks of islands, elevated only a few feet above the general level of the sea. There is a chain of small islands along the coast of Holland inhabited by a people we call Frisians. Every few years a storm sweeps over their islands causing great damage, but I suppose they think they have the finest country in the world. By the way, these Frisians are a most interesting people to the scholar. I might say their language is now the purest representative of Old Saxon; and the Saxons who invaded England, when the Romans left, were near relatives to the Frisians.

' Now I will show you just one more scene in Holland. These numerous canals that we have talked about are generally frozen over in winter, and as

FISHING IN HOLLAND.

a consequence the Dutch are noted for their skating; and then they may be seen cutting small holes in the ice and fishing. In short, Holland is one of the most interesting countries of Europe.

"Right to the south of Holland is the Kingdom of Belgium. Traveling in the convenient fashion that we are, we will just suppose ourselves set down at Brussels. Find it on the map, Burt; and, Henry, what does the name make you think of?"

"Why, I don't know—is it Brussels carpet, uncle?"

"That is it. Brussels is celebrated, among other things, for its carpets. Now Belgium, as you know, is a very small kingdom; in its present form it is very recent, only some sixty years old. In ancient history it is often spoken of as Flanders, and its history is all mixed up with Holland. But its capital, Brussels, is one of the pleasantest cities in all Europe. It is noted for its fine public buildings. I have here a plate giving us an idea of some of the principal ones. The one at the top is the Palace of Justice; it is a most magnificent building. Then we have a view of one of the churches in the center, and at the bottom is the Exchange."

"And what are those two statues?" asked Burt.

"They are for two Counts, Egmont and Horn, put to death in 1568 by Duke Alva. If you want your blood to boil, you read of the terrible doings of the Spaniards under Duke Alva in the Netherlands—that is to say, in what is now Holland and Belgium."

"I wish, uncle, you would tell us just a little about this Duke Alva, for I have heard of him before," said Burt.

"I scarcely have time to tell you very much about him," replied Uncle George, "but perhaps I can give you an outline. You know, probably, that Holland and Belgium are often called the Netherlands. In the sixteenth century these formed a part of the territory of Spain. Philip II. of Spain was a most bigoted ruler, and he was determined to crush out all liberty of conscience in the Netherlands. For this purpose he sent Duke Alva there. He was a very able military general, but was extremely cruel and blood-thirsty. Great was the alarm in the Netherlands when he made his appearance at the head of a formidable Spanish army. No great resistance could be offered to him, though William the Silent that we were talking about a moment ago, almost single-handed, withstood him. His council, which from its severity was called the "Council of Blood," was a terrible thing. I have seen it estimated that in the six years he was in the Netherlands he caused eighteen thousand people to be put to death! That seems almost incredible, don't it? But the least suspicion, especially if the suspected person were rich, was sufficient to condemn him to death. The two Counts that Burt asked about were

BRUSSELS.

among the first to fall. They had done nothing worthy of death, but were greatly liked by the people. But I think we had better find something pleasanter to talk about."

"Haven't you a picture of this duke, uncle, so that we can see what he looks like?" inquired Nettie.

DUKE OF ALVA AT BRUSSELS.

"I have no picture in this collection, but—let me think—ah yes, in this book" (taking one from the library) "is a view of him when he had just arrived in Brussels, deposing the Duchess of Parma, who was then regent. Notice his cold, haughty looks. But now, leaving the past, do any of you remember any event of great interest in modern history that happened near Brussels?"

No one could recall it until Uncle George mentioned that it was a battle in which Napoleon was engaged; and then they all, with the possible exception of Henry, thought of Waterloo.

"The Field of Waterloo," said Uncle George, "is only about twelve miles from Brussels, and is one of the sights of the place. The mound you

THE FIELD OF WATERLOO.

see is about two hundred feet high; on its top is a bronze figure of a lion, the emblem of Belgium. As you all know, this was the final battle of Napoleon's life; here he was finally overthrown. When I was there," continued Uncle George after a brief pause, "some scattered lines of Scott's poem kept running through my mind. I will try and recall them for you. They are taken from several different verses, but I think they go well together, and they express a sad truth:

VIEWS IN BERLIN, "UNTER DEN LINDEN."

> Look forth, once more, with softened heart,
> Ere from the field of fame we part.
> Thou canst not name one tender tie
> But here dissolved its relics lie!
> Still, in story and in song
> For many an age remembered long,
> Shall live the towers of Hougoumont
> And fields of Waterloo."

"Uncle, what does the country look like?" broke in Henry.

"Well, of course, the scenery changes considerably; but as you enter Germany from France you will notice the grain fields stretching away on both sides; then plains with herds of cattle and flocks of sheep tended by shepherds; little villages with clusters of dark and cheerless houses built of stone and mortar, with homely red-tile roofs; wide white roads, level as marble floors, some of them sheltered on each side by rows of poplar trees. Now and then you see the ruins of some old castle on a distant hill top; but what you will also see is the women of the poorer class, bronze-featured, scantily dressed, toiling in the field like so many cattle. Nowhere will you see fences. What we have been considering form the smaller kingdoms of Teutonic Europe. We will now turn our attention to Germany proper, and the easiest way of getting at this part of our work is to consider ourselves in Berlin, and then we can make trips to other parts of this great empire. When you are in Berlin, you must remember you are in the capital of probably the strongest single power in Europe; and yet the present German Empire is a very modern affair.

"In this plate we have a collection of views of the finest street in Berlin; it is known all over as 'Unter den Linden' (Under the Lindens). In the first picture, in the corner, you see the general plan of the street. It is about two hundred feet wide. There is a magnificent walk in the center of the street, bordered by chestnut, linden, and other trees. It is about a mile long, running east and west, and lined with some of the finest buildings in Europe. In the lowest cut you see the beautiful gate at the western end surmounted by a triumphal car. That is the Brandenberg Gate. Napoleon carried it to Paris with him, but the Prussians brought it back after the battle of Waterloo."

"Probably the French thought they were going to get it back in the last war," said Burt.

"Perhaps they did, but the gate was not in much danger.   But through
that gate came the victorious German army after the war, with bluff old King
William riding at its head, with Bismarck, Von Moltke, and his generals at his
side.   You can imagine the scene along that famous street on that memorable
day.   At the eastern end of the Linden we come to a fine equestrian statue

FREDERICK THE GREAT'S STATUE

of Frederick the Great (we will talk more about him by and by), and here
we have a picture of it.   The pedestal proper is twenty-five feet high; then
comes all those figures you see on horseback—they are life size.   In the panel
above are represented different stages in the life of Frederick; then comes
the figure of Frederick on his horse.   It is very natural.

"After passing this statue we come to a square known as the 'Opera Place.' It contains one or two palaces, the Royal Library, and the university for which Berlin is deservedly famous; more than three thousand students attend lectures at the university.

"Passing that square we come to the very center of the city. The River Spree goes winding through the city, and we cross one of its arms by a very

THE SCHLOSS BRIDGE.

fine bridge called the Schloss Brucke—that is, the Castle Bridge, and find ourselves in what is known as the Lustgarten.

"What is that big building with a dome on it?" asked Burt.

"That is the cathedral in which a great many ancestors of the royal family are buried."

"And what is that building with such a number of pillars in front of it?" asked Nettie.

"That is the Old Museum, one of the most imposing buildings in Berlin, and the ground in front of it is beautifully laid out."

"And there is the statue of that king on horseback?" said Henry.

"No; that is the statue of another king, Frederick William III. The two great kings of Prussia, by the way, are Frederick the Great and William I. The one made Prussia a formidable power; it was the good fortune of the other to be King of Prussia when German Unity was brought

FREDERICK THE GREAT.

about, and so he was the first Emperor of United Germany. I have here a picture of this famous Frederick; and if you want to read something that will interest and excite you, I advise you to read some good account of his life. Almost single-handed he fought against France, Austria, and Russia, who were determined to divide Prussia among themselves. But after seven years of fighting they gave it up as a bad job.

"Emperor William was fortunate in his reign. He personally did not do as much as Frederick, but he called around him some of the greatest men of modern times; such as Von Moltke, the great general, and Bismarck, the statesman. It was these men, quite as much as his own ability, that made

POTSDAM.

him Emperor of United Germany. He was crowned Emperor in Paris, near the conclusion of the last war with France.

Henry probably expressed the thoughts of all when he exclaimed, as Uncle George concluded, "I'll bet he felt good then." But, as Uncle George said, he had a right to feel "good."

"Potsdam is only sixteen miles from Berlin. It is beautifully situated on an island. Here we have a view of the town. It is noted for its beautiful palace, one of the finest in Europe, built by Frederick at the close of the Seven Years' War to show Europe that he had plenty of money left. In the

church vault lies the body of this great warrior, in a plain metal coffin, by
the side of his eccentric father that I haven't time to tell you about now.
When Napoleon was in Berlin, after his great victory over Prussia, he paid a
visit to this vault. Bowing his knees, he said, 'Hadst thou been alive I
should never have been here.' But he carried away with him the sword of
Frederick which lay on the coffin. It was never known what became of it,
though you may be sure the Prussians searched for it after the battle of
Waterloo."

"I wonder what made him do it," said Nettie. "I suppose, though, he
thought it would be an interesting relic," she added.

"Now, tell us about the palace you spoke of," said Henry.

"Perhaps I ought to have said palaces," said Uncle George, "for there
are some five royal residences in and around Potsdam. There is the Old
Palace where Frederick the Great lived most of his time when not engaged
in war. It contains the furniture which he used, all scratched by the claws
of his dogs, for he was very fond of dogs; and there is his writing table
covered with ink, the room where he used to dine, etc. Not very far from
there is the Palace of Sans Souci, and in this plate we have a collection of
views of this palace and the grounds. You can imagine how beautiful it
must be. In the palace is the room in which the great Frederick died; it
contains the clock which he used to wind with his own hand, and which we
are assured stopped just at the moment he died."

"Do you believe it did, uncle?" asked Willie, in rather a skeptical tone.

"Well, I wont vouch for that, Willie. In sight-seeing, as in some other
things, there are many statements you must take on faith; if you go to
inquiring and doubting, you will spoil many a little romance There is the
clock, at any rate, stopped at twenty minutes past two.

"By the way, right to one side of the grounds' of this palace stands a
famous windmill. Frederick tried to buy it, as he wanted to pull it down, so
as to extend his grounds. The miller refused to sell; whereupon the King
went to law about it, but the courts decided against him. But here again
the suspicious traveler cannot help wondering whether the court did not
have a private intimation from the King how to decide, since Frederick
erected for the miller a larger mill as a monument of Prussian justice. The
whole thing looks suspiciously like a well-worked 'ad.,' as we would say in
this country."

PALACE OF SAN SOUCI.

9

"Then you don't believe it, uncle?" said Burt.

"Oh, yes, I believe the facts just as they are stated; but in those days courts would have been a little careful how they decided against the 'divine rights of kings.' However, there is a good story about Frederick. He was riding in the royal coach and observed a crowd trying to read a placard

LUTHER AND MELANCHTHON.

posted on the wall. He found it to be a cartoon on himself. Frederick did not get mad and order a lot of people arrested; on the contrary, he coolly ordered the placard to be put a little lower down so the people could see it better. But we must go back to Berlin and start on our travels again. There is one place about sixty miles, a little to the southwest of Berlin, that it will pay us to stop at. That is Wittenberg. It is the place where Martin Luther started in his work. Of course, it is not necessary to tell you who Luther was."

" Was he born at Wittenberg?" asked Nettie.

" No, he was born at Eisleben, but was professor at Wittenberg. This part of Prussia (pointing to Saxony on the map) was the home of the Reformation. The German Empire, as you know, is an immense great one, and so we will devote a little time to Southern Germany. Bavaria is perhaps the most important of the Southern German States. Although it is part of the German Empire, it is still an organized kingdom of itself, and has some

MUNICH.

especial privileges. Its capital is Munich, and there we will suppose ourselves to have arrived, and here is our first view of Munich; and Munich, we might remark, is one of the most interesting cities in Europe. It is rich in art treasures, palaces, and public buildings."

"Is that a bridge?" asked Burt.

"Yes, that is a bridge over the Iser. Do you know of any poem about the River Iser?"

As usual, it was Nettie who responded by reciting:

> "On Linden when the sun was low
> . All bloodless lay the untrodden snow,
> And dark as winter was the flow
> Of Iser, rolling rapidly."

"That is it, and I can say that one of the most interesting sights in Munich is to stand on one of these old bridges and watch the boiling, foaming waters as they go rushing by underneath. Hohenlinden, where the battle was fought, to which this poem refers, is about twenty miles east of Munich.

THE MARIENPLATZ.

"This place is not so very old, that is, as age counts in Europe, since it only dates back some seven or eight centuries. But Munich has been entirely made over, so to speak, within the present century. Here is a view of one of the squares in Munich. It is named from the pillar with a statue on top that you see in the corner, the 'Marienplatz.' The pillar is of red marble with a bronze statue of the Virgin surmounting it. It commemorates a victory gained over two hundred and fifty years ago. The fountain that you see is the scene of one of those curious senseless customs that you are continually meeting in Europe. Every young butcher apprentice, when he takes his freedom—that is to say, when he becomes a full-fledged butcher—has to go and jump into the fountain."

"I wouldn't do that," said Henry.

"I guess you would if you were in Munich, Henry. As usual, there is a story about it. Once on a time, some two or three centuries ago, there was a great plague in Munich. When it died away it was difficult to convince the people that the city was a safe place to live in, so the butchers of the city marched in procession to the fountain, and one after another plunged in. When it was seen that no evil effects followed from their bath, why the people in general concluded that it was once more safe to live in Munich. Thus the custom started, and in Europe customs are followed with great fidelity.

"Now I could spend the rest of the evening, if necessary, in talking about Munich, but we cannot give it so much space. There are palaces, museums, and picture galleries almost without number. To give you an idea of how money has been spent by the kings of Bavaria, I will say that in one palace is a bed—in which Napoleon once slept, by the way—the drapery and coverlid of which are so richly wrought with gold embroidery that they are said to have cost nearly three hundred and fifty thousand dollars.

"Of one institution I will speak, although I have no picture to illustrate it—that is the cemetery. Attached to the cemetery is a building in which the bodies are placed for an indefinite time before burial. Signaling apparatuses are connected with them in such a way that, should there be any life left in the body, the slightest motion will ring a bell and summon an attendant. You can look in through the window. Here is an account of the impressions produced on one writer speaking of the little children he saw therein."

This time also Willie read: "There must have been fifteen or twenty of them. They were lying outside of their caskets on soft little cushions or blankets of rich material, and in their dainty white muslin or silk dresses, trimmed with handsome embroidered edgings and laces, looked as if they had been to a children's dress party, and, overcome with fatigue, had fallen asleep. Several were in reclining positions, propped up with cushions, with wreaths of handsome artificial or real flowers placed on their heads, and little bouquets in their hands. Two or three were so covered with floral decorations they looked as if they were sleeping in beds of flowers. Such a picture seemed to rob death of its terrors."

"We will stop at one more city of Bavaria; that is Nuremberg. Here is a view of the walls, for Nuremberg has much to remind us of the past. Our own poet, Longfellow, has a poem on Nuremberg that expresses the facts:

NUREMBERG—CITY WALLS.

Quaint old town of toil and traffic, quaint old town of art and song,
Memories haunt thy pointed gables, like the rooks that round them throng;
Memories of the Middle Ages, when the emperors, rough and bold
Had their dwelling in thy castle, time defying, centuries old.

"The walls of Nuremberg are about three miles and a half in circumference, and so the city presents the appearance of a place in the Middle Ages. The moat still exists, one hundred feet wide, crossed by draw-bridges, and could still be flooded with water; but now the bottom of the moat is covered with market gardens. On the wall a large number of the nearly four hundred towers that once guarded it, still remain. It has walls like Chester, in England, you notice."

"Were the Romans ever there, uncle?" inquired Henry.

"No; the Roman Empire included very little of what is now Teutonic Europe. It was the various Germanic people which finally overthrew the Roman Empire; but for many centuries after the fall of that empire, cities were surrounded with walls.

"You notice on the map a little river running; it is called the Pegnitz, as it cuts the town completely in two. Of course, there are bridges crossing it. In this view we have such a bridge, and you must notice the houses rising right up out of the water."

"Is Nuremberg a large place, uncle?" asked Burt.

BRIDGE AT NUREMBERG.

"It is the second city in Bavaria, and has a population of nearly one hundred and fifty thousand. It is very interesting to the historian. The castle of the old city was for a long time a favorite place of residence with the German emperors. Frederick Barbarossa once lived there. When you read history you will learn what a celebrated person he was. Popular superstition thinks that Barbarossa is not dead, but sleeping the time away in a cave, and when the right time comes he will make his appearance."

"How funny. Do they really believe it, uncle?" asked Henry.

"I guess not," said Uncle George with a smile, "but nearly every country has some legend of a sleeping person, like our Rip Van Winkle I

CHURCH OF ST. LAWRENCE.

saw you reading the other day. Nuremberg has a wonderful fountain, and is noted for its beautiful churches. Here I have a view of one of them. As Longfellow says:

Everywhere I see around me rise the wondrous world of art,
Fountains wrought with richest sculpture standing in the common mart;
And above cathedral doorways saints and bishops carved in stone
By a former age commissioned as apostles to our own.

"The Church of St. Lawrence, shown in the cut, is regarded as one of the most beautiful in Europe. The carvings around the altar are very

beautiful, in reference to which Longfellow still continues in his exquisite
verse:

> In the church of sainted Lawrence stands a pyx of sculpture rare,
> Like the foamy sheaf of fountains rising through the painted air."

"Is there any story about that fountain?" asked Henry, keeping in mind
the fountain at Munich, but Uncle George told him he did not know of any.

THE BURGOMASTER.

"Now, before leaving Germany, we will talk a little about some peculiarities of German life. I will show you this cut of a Bavarian Burgomaster.
That is the village official. In Germany we quickly discover that the government has the controlling interest in about everything that is going on. The
government educates, drills, and marches the people; looks after their reli-

gion, and must be consulted with in the question of marriage. It runs the railroads and telegraph lines, and owns most of the forest land. But, in return for all this fostering care, it unmercifully taxes the people. Take the little Kingdom of Wurtemberg, smaller, as far as size is concerned, than the State of Massachusetts, yet it costs over twelve million dollars annually to run the government. They pay the king, for instance, over four hundred thousand dollars. Some day Europe will make up its mind that it can get along without its royal families."

"What will happen then?" asked Burt.

SWABIANS.

"The change will almost certainly be accompanied by a terrible storm. At present emigration affords some relief to the almost overburdened people. I read, only in this morning's paper, that from one German port over five thousand emigrants sailed for this country. You must know that in a country where the kings build palaces without number, and indulge in the luxury of bed-clothes costing three hundred and fifty thousand dollars, that nihilism and socialism are bound to increase. The government may succeed in smothering or smoothing it over for the time being, but the explosion must come some time.

"Here is a common-place picture of people living in that part of Germany called Swabia; that is in the southwestern part of Germany around Stuttgart.

In that part of Germany we come upon the Black Forest, where we find so many stories and legends."

"Uncle, what about the Black Forest? I have heard of it somewhere before," said Burt.

"That Black Forest is a remnant of the great forest that once covered all of Central Europe. The Romans called it the Hercynian Forest. They had little relish for exploring it. Cæsar, in his Commentaries, mentions it as being inhabited with all sorts of fierce and savage tribes. During the Middle Ages this was inhabited by half civilized tribes, and long continued to be the home of bands of robbers. And at the present day, as I have said, the people are very backward, and consequently superstitious, and believe the many stories they hear of fairies and goblins."

"Tell us a story, uncle," exclaimed Henry.

After a short pause Uncle George said: "I will only relate a short one; it will give you an idea of what they are like. You must know that the Black Forest people believe in the existence of a very mischievous elf called Poppele, who delights in playing all manner of practical though good-natured jokes. He treats all alike, whether they are saint or sinner. Once upon a time an abbess, celebrated for her piety, was riding in a coach from one convent to another, when, all of a sudden, the carriage stuck fast. In vain the coachman tried whipping and coaxing to have the horses go ahead. They could not budge the carriage. At length the coachman, getting impatient, went to the carriage door.

"'Madam,' he cried, 'what is to be done? Will you get out?'

"'Impossible,' cried the holy abbess.

"'Then, madam, will you permit me to swear a few oaths? That may do some good.'

"But the good abbess could not hear of that; she shuddered at the very thought; but after a weary waiting she thought differently about it, and called out of the window to the coachman, 'If you must swear, proceed; we must get agoing somehow.' And, it is added, she herself set the example. At this explosion from the pious abbess there was heard a shriek of laughter, and Poppele let go the wheel he had been holding all the while, and the carriage proceeded merrily on its way.

"So much for that particular story," concluded Uncle George, "and it is wonderful how many stories of this character you hear; and we are not surprised to know they believe in witchcraft, and many such absurd things the rest of the world have forgotten."

We are not sure but the club would have preferred some more stories, but Uncle George said this would give them a sample of the numerous

ROMANS WARRING WITH THE GERMANS.

stories to be heard in Swabia, and he wanted to tell them a little early German history. "I said but a moment ago," he resumed, "that the Roman Empire included in its bounds but a small part of what is Teutonic Europe. Rome attained her zenith of prosperity at the commencement of the Christian era. A famous battle was fought by the Roman General Varus somewhere in the section of Germany we are now talking about, and the Romans were completely defeated. This picture is from a painting supposed to represent that battle. After that the Germans were never afraid of Roman conquest; in 'fact, they were soon the aggressors.

"The primitive Germans who defeated the Romans were a sturdy race of people. They were distinguished by their lofty stature, their robust limbs, their fair complexion, and flowing hair. They have never yet had justice done to them in the pages of history. All our early notices of them come from the description of their enemies—the Romans. We are only just

PRIMITIVE WORSHIP AMONG THE GERMANS.

now learning how much our civilization owes to them. Of course, at that early time they were pagans, and had their Druid priesthood that you know I spoke about the first night."

"Talking about Wales," broke in Burt.

"Yes, exactly. Well, here is a cut which represents worship among them. They met in the forests. Remember what I said about their long hair and fair complexion."

"What are those things those men have on their heads?" inquired Willie.

"Like all partially civilized people their chiefs liked to wear head-dress,

ALPHONSE DE NEUVILLE.

GERMAN WOMEN DEFENDING THEIR WAGON CASTLES AGAINST
THE ROMANS.

significant of their name or rank. It was these people who finally commenced their inroads on Rome. Our large picture represents the women defending their rude Wagon Castles against a band of Roman soldiers.

"Well, the Romans passed away, the German people became Christianized, and finally we come to what is known as the Age of Feudalism and Chivalry in Europe. Now, this was an important period in European history, and, of course, of the early history of the present great German States

FEUDAL CASTLE AT ROUEN.

of Europe. Owing to many causes, the chiefs grew into powerful lords and built themselves great castles, such as the one shown in this cut.

"You see it is surrounded by a stream of water called a moat; a draw-bridge led across the moat. Before the invention of fire-arms such a castle as this was a secure place of retreat. This picture properly represents the Feudal Age, and I might remark that you find many remains along the Rhine of Feudal times."

"You know you told me once to look up about Feudal times," exclaimed Burt. "I found out a good deal about it, but you just now spoke about Chivalry. What was that?"

"I am afraid," replied Uncle George, "that it would be extremely difficult to give you a fair idea of Chivalry without taking up too much time.
You had better look that up, too; but I will tell you of some of their customs.
I have here a view of a knight attended by his squires.. Knighthood, I might
remark, was the great institution of Chivalry. We, at the present day, see a
great deal in their ideas to laugh about, but it seemed earnest enough to them."

KNIGHTHOOD.

Here Uncle George handed a book to Ida, who read the following extract
about life in the Middle Ages: "Strange and picturesque sights were to be
seen. The young knight, full of ambition to make himself a name, rode
along accompanied by his squire anxious to find some adventure to distin-
guish himself, or to meet with another like-minded knight with whom to
cross his lance. The feudal lord, with his armed retainers, was to be seen
riding forth from his castle, and hunting parties scoured the woods. The
gentleman would ride by in silks and velvets, in plumed hat and enameled
belt, attended by his servants. The minstrel, in gay coat, sang snatches of
lays as he wandered along, from hall to castle. The more stately group of

TOURNAMENT.

knights and squires hurrying along were on their way to attend some tournament."

"Uncle, wont you tell us something about the tournaments? I have read about them, but what were they?" broke in Nettie.

"Tournaments were great institutions in the days of Chivalry. They were the military games of the age; they were courteous battles between two parties of armed knights. In Germany the

A TOURNAMENT.

ENTRANCE TO THE TOURNAMENT.

country was divided off into districts, in which tournaments were held by rotation. They were in those days what races are in our day. All Europe, and especially Germany, delighted in these contests. In these views you see the knight all armed entering the lists, as it was called, attended by his servants, called squires and pages. And you also see the contest going on. The combat was conducted under very strict rules."

"Are they fighting in real earnest?" asked Henry.

"Yes, they are earnest enough. However, the weapons were so arranged that not much danger was to be feared from that source; but, of course, the sport was dangerous. You see I have here a large view of a tournament. Of course, knighthood has passed away; but you all know we have many bodies of knights of different names still existing. They keep alive a dim memory of that earlier time."

" I read about knights and squires in ' Sancho Panza,' " said Burt, with a laugh, as he recalled the funny incidents of that book.

" Yes, and, by the way, that book raised such a laugh that it about put an end to Chivalry.   I see I have here a picture of one of the most famous

BARBAROSSA ASKING AID OF KING HENRY.

emperors of ancient Germany, Barbarossa.   I spoke of him just a moment ago.   He was one of the crusaders, and this represents him asking the aid of the king of England for one of his crusades.   He is quite a popular hero, and, as I said, there is a story told about him that he is sleeping his life away in a cave surrounded by his valiant knights, and some day he is to awaken to new life and lead his people on to new victories.   I have been

talking about old Germany. I see I have here a view of one the most celebrated cathedrals in Europe. It belongs to both old and new Germany; for,
though begun some six centuries ago, it is not yet fully completed. The
Germany of to-day is perhaps the strongest power in Europe. She has been
victorious in all her recent wars, and is now a united country."

COLOGNE CATHEDRAL.

But at this point Aunt Mary entered the room, and her entrance meant
that it was already getting late, and so Uncle George closed up the books.
There was the usual amount of informal talk. Probably all the club were
glad to hear the announcement that the next trip would be to France.

CHAPTER V.

FRANCE AND SPAIN.

THE fourth meeting of the club fell on Washington's birthday, and as Uncle George was going to talk to them about France, it occurred to him that it would not be a bad plan to introduce the evening's work by making some general remarks on the peculiar relation between this country and France at that critical time in our history. And it is not at all strange that one or two of the older children had also thought of the same thing. At school they had public exercises; and orations and essays, having for their subject-matter Washington and the Revolution, had been the order of the day.

So when the club gathered in the library, it is not surprising that Nettie's first remark was: "Uncle, I want to ask you a few questions about this country and France at the time of the Revolution. What made France help us?"

And in reply Uncle George told them about the troubled condition of affairs in Europe at that time. He recalled to their mind how much trouble France had had with England for almost a century previous to our Revolution. And so it was not strange that France looked favorably upon the colonies from the start. "It is rather of a surprise to the average American," continued he, "to find what a strong hold France had in what is now the Mississippi Valley long before the English had made any settlements there. They had explored our great lakes, and sailed up and down the Mississippi, the Illinois, and Ohio rivers, and had established a chain of forts all through the interior. You know it was in an attempt to capture old Fort Du Quesne, where Pittsburgh now stands, that first brought Washington to public notice. Had his advance been followed, Braddock would probably not have sustained his terrible defeat. But we must return to our regular work for the evening.

"The Revolutionary times have long since passed away, and our country is now rich and prosperous. France has passed through some ups and downs since then, but is still a most interesting country to visit. The American traveler ought never to forget how greatly that country helped us in our time of trouble. You all know who the Marquis de La Fayette was. I have here a fine view of that gallant young Frenchman."

" He came over here and helped us, didn't he?" said Henry.

"Yes, indeed, and most splendid assistance it was, too. Just think of this wealthy and titled young Frenchman leaving wife, home, and native land to help us, before he was twenty years of age. His arrival in this country produced a great sensation. Nearly fifty years afterwards, when he was an old man, he visited our country, at the earnest invitation of Congress, and his tour resembled a triumphant procession from city to city. Our government sent a ship to bring him over, and named it the Brandywine, in memory of an important battle he fought near Phila-

LA FAYETTE.

delphia. And only recently, when we had our Yorktown Centennial, one of the guests of our country that Congress especially invited was a young lieutenant in the French army, a relative of the gallant La Fayette."

"What made him want to come and help us?" asked Willie. "Was it just for a good time?"

"No, the whole life of the man shows that his influence was always on the side of the weak and oppressed. No man would have held the love and confidence of Washington, as he did, who was not a good man. Our representative at Paris, Benjamin Franklin, impressed him greatly. Franklin, whose picture I have here, was greatly liked in France, and contributed in no small degree in inducing that country to help us in our Revolution."

"One question more, if you please, uncle," said Burt. "Why is it that the United States appear to have forgotten this, and in the last war we almost all sided with Germany?"

BENJAMIN FRANKLIN.

"Well, Burt, France has largely herself to blame for that. She seemed to think that she held a mortgage on us afterwards. Even in Washington's life-time we came near being drawn into a war with France. But in her last war with Germany, France was so clearly to blame that we could not support her claim. Paris," continued Uncle George, opening a book, "is probably the gayest capital of modern times. It is not the largest, but it is a very inter-

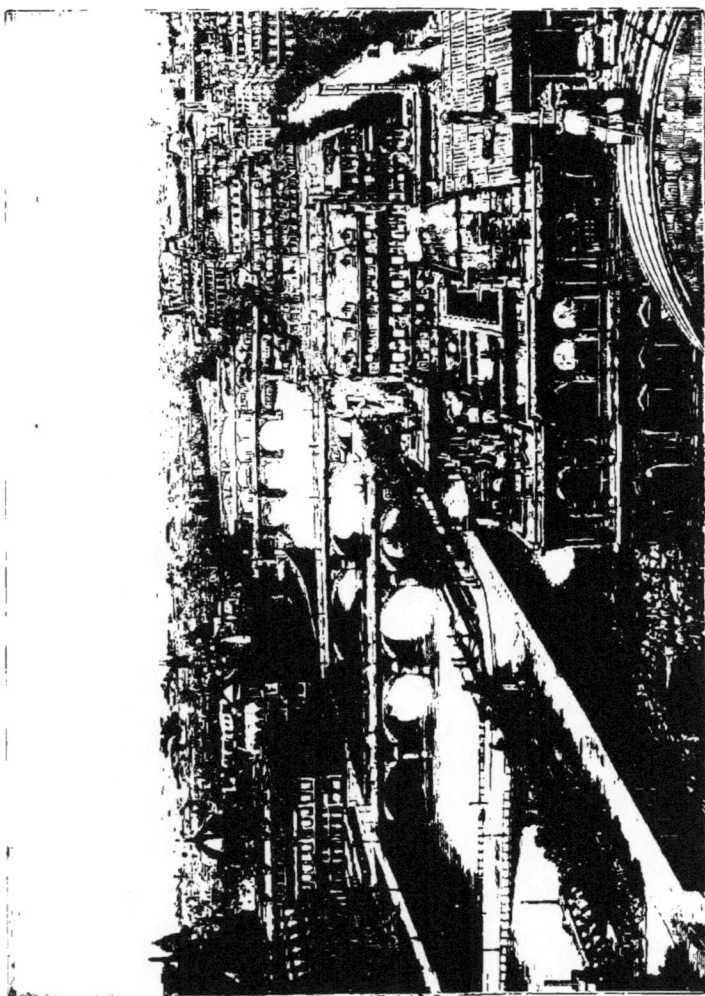

PARIS.

esting place to visit. I have here a general view of the city, showing seven of the bridges over the River Seine.

"The river is only a few hundred feet wide, though there is quite a volume of water flowing through it, and you notice the sides are what are called quayed. There are some twenty-seven bridges crossing it. Paris, you know, is a great big place, having about two million inhabitants. You can

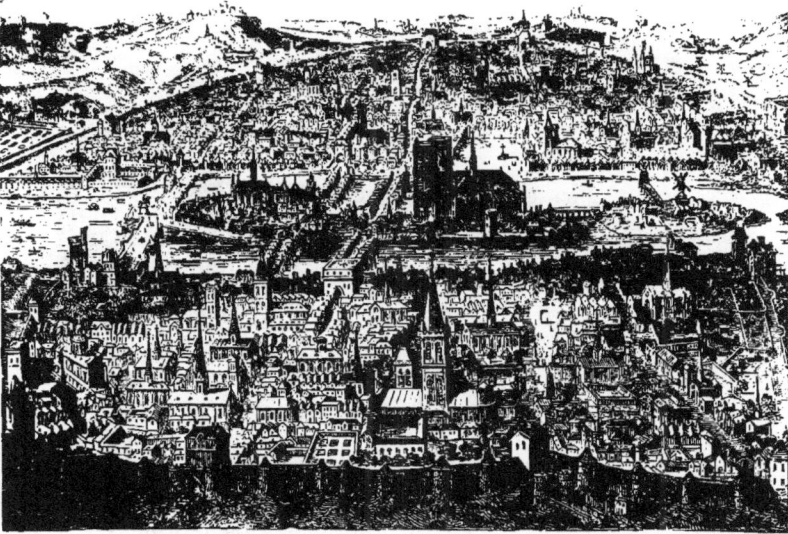

PARIS OF THE SEVENTEENTH CENTURY.

not begin to understand Paris until you have spent some time in studying it. I hardly know where to begin in describing it. Perhaps, by way of a little historical sketch, I might as well show you this cut of Paris in the seventeenth century. You must notice the walls and the island in the river. On that island was made the first settlement in the vicinity of Paris."

"I think I read somewhere that there was a city there before Roman times," said Burt.

"Yes, and the name Paris shows how geographical places keep alive the names of long-lost people. The settlement of the *Parisii* tribe was on that island. But from the fourth century down Paris has been one of the noted places of Europe. The city walls have been leveled, and in their stead are the beautiful boulevards comprising the very finest streets in the world. But we must now examine some of the principal sights of Paris.

"Once no less than sixty acres in the very heart of Paris, on the right bank of the River Seine, were occupied by a magnificent group of palaces known as the Louvre and the Tuileries. The former is shown in this cut.

VIEW OF THE LOUVRE.

The historian," continued Mr. Adams after a brief pause, "takes a melancholy interest in contemplating the scenes that the walls of this palace have witnessed. For more than a hundred years it was the favorite residence of the Bourbon kings. There beautiful Mary, Queen of Scots, lived for a while as the bride of Francis II. There Catherine de Medici planned the terrible St. Bartholomew massacre. Henry of Navarre lived there, and the great Richelieu laid the foundation of France's greatness. Since then that has become the great museum of France. There are literally miles of paintings and most interesting collections of antiquities.

"The other great pile of royal buildings standing on this space were known as the Tuileries. They were destroyed by the mob in 1871. Here were enacted the principal scenes of the stormy close of Louis XVI.'s life."

F. LIX.

LOUIS XVI. BIDS ADIEU TO HIS FAMILY ON THE POINT OF DEPARTING TO THE
PLACE DE LA CONCORD TO BE GUILLOTINED.   171

"I remember how I cried when I read the life of Marie Antoinette," said Nettie. "I think it was just awful."

Uncle George only smiled thoughtfully as he remarked that "mobs are always cruel," though they may have most substantial cause for complaint."

"If that was such a nice palace, what made them burn it?" asked Henry.

"That was the work of another mob, the Commune. After their terrible defeat at the hands of the Prussians, in their last war, there was so

PLACE DE LA CONCORDE.

much disappointment that once more the worst elements of the city got the upper hand; and they committed all sorts of excesses. The beautiful Louvre we looked at a moment ago had a very narrow escape. One wing of the building was burned, and many thousand volumes of rare and costly works were destroyed before the government troops arrived on the scene.

"We have in this view a picture of one of the grandest public places to be found in any city of Europe, the Place de la Concorde. The views in all directions from the center of this square are charming. Speaking of it at night, it may be compared to an immense open-air theater in the midst of an enormous, brilliantly illuminated garden. To the one side are the magnificent gardens of the Tuileries, and in other directions open out most charming streets. At the four corners of the square are eight pedestals, bearing allegorical figures representing eight of the principal cities of France. And, by the way, in July you may witness a really touching sight. You know that as a result of the Prussian war Strasburg became a German city. Its statue is one of the eight. On the day of the July *fete* the statue of that city is literally loaded with wreaths in sorrow for its loss. Doubtless all France hopes—but with hopes ever growing fainter—to one day put on that statue garlands emblematic of joy at its return to France."

"Uncle, what about that great, tall pillar?" asked Burt.

"That is known as the Obelisk of Luxor. It was brought from Egypt. It used to stand before the Temple at Thebes, and was erected by a king who lived more than fifteen hundred years before Christ. It has seen some wonderful changes in the world's history, hasn't it? Just think; its native country, Egypt, which was then the center of civilization and culture, is now but a province of another empire—a people at that time unknown. The great Roman Empire has come and gone; Europe has passed from barbarism to the height of civilization; a new world has been discovered; and thus we could go on, and not begin to exhaust the list of wonderful things that have happened in the course of time since that pillar was first erected at Thebes."

"How did it ever get to Paris?" inquired Ida.

"Napoleon had it brought to France as a memento of his conquest in Egypt. But we must return to our subject.

"The name of this place, I said, was Concorde; but perhaps a better name would be the 'Place of Blood.' For terrible scenes have been witnessed here. The guillotine was put up here in the Reign of Terror. Here the unfortunate King Louis XVI. was beheaded, and a few weeks later his once beautiful Queen Marie Antoinette. And here came the beautiful enthusiast, Charlotte Corday, proud of having slain the tyrant Marat. And thus the Reign of Terror continued until finally the leaders of it were themselves put to death."

"What are they doing in the picture?" asked Henry.

"Charlotte Corday, Henry, had killed Marat, one of the tyrants that I may speak about soon. She, of course, was condemned to death. Her lover

CHARLOTTE CORDAY BEING SUMMONED TO EXECUTION.

T. SCHUBERT.

175

was painting her picture when the officers came to lead her away to execution. But now let us turn to a more attractive subject. Running in a northeasterly direction from the Place de la Concorde is the beautiful Avenue of Champs Elysees. This avenue is a mile and a quarter in length. There are rows of trees and bitumen walks twelve feet wide with beautiful borders.

FOUNTAIN IN THE CHAMPS ELYSEES.

Easy spring chairs are provided for the multitude. In fine weather this is the favorite spot for all classes. From morning until far into the night it is thronged with the elegant vehicles of the rich. On every side there are beautiful groves; here and there fountains surrounded with flower-beds such as is shown in this cut. At night, when all is lighted up by the thousand lamps, the scene is entrancing. But on *fete* days, when every building is

11

transformed into a palace of fire, and every tree into a pyramid of lights—well, I will leave it to your imagination how grand it is."

Judging from expressions of delight, imagination was doing considerable—especially in Henry's case—to realize the scene. Turning the page, Uncle George continued:

"We have only made a beginning on the public buildings of Paris, but we must hurry on. Another palace is known as the Luxembourg Palace. It

PALACE OF THE LUXEMBOURG.

was built by Marie de Medici, Queen of Henry IV. But she did not enjoy her palace very much, as you will see when you read history. During the French Revolution Bonaparte came here after his triumphant campaign in Italy, and was received by the exultant directors; and in the circle of those who pressed forward to greet him was the fair Josephine Beauharnais, who was destined to enjoy his triumphs with him."

"Yes, and it was just mean how he treated her, too," broke in Nettie, "and it just served him right the way his fortune changed after he divorced her," she added, rather spitefully.

"I guess you are about right, said Uncle George, smiling.

"Here is one more palace that we will glance at. That is the Palais Royal shown in this view. It was burned in the mob days of 1871, but has since

PALAIS ROYAL.

been restored. It was built by the great statesman, Richelieu. In the days of Louis XVI., the glories of this palace and the court held there rivaled those of Versailles, about which we will talk soon. Some years ago the beautiful gardens of this palace made it the center of attraction; but its glory has now departed for the Champs Elysees and the beautiful boulevards. This garden, too, is linked with the memory of Revolutionary days. Here is where the movement really started that led to the fall of the Bastile."

"Uncle," said Burt, as Mr. Adams ceased speaking, "if it is not out of place, I wish you would tell us a little about the French Revolution."

LOUIS XIV.

"To fully answer that question would require far more time than we can give it. I will only give a general idea. Louis XIV., whose picture I have here, had a very long and, to outward appearances, a very brilliant reign, but then began that train of events which led to the great explosion toward the end of the eighteenth century. It was the first recitation of the lesson which the nobility of Europe seems not to have learned even yet. The king and the nobility of France seem to have thought that the common people had no rights whatever, and acted accordingly. This costly error was atoned for in blood in the reign of Louis XVI. It is unfortunate that, when a storm of this kind arises, much innocent suffering necessarily accompanies it.

"Now I have here two scenes of the French Revolution. The first is the storming of the Bastile. This was one of the first acts of the Revolution. It was the prison of Paris where were confined the State prisoners. The second scene is the execu-

STORMING OF THE BASTILE.

tion of Louis XVI. It took place in the beautiful Place de la Concorde. The King was calm and dignified to the last."

"They cut off his head the way they did that English king, Charles I.," said Henry.

"Yes; but the revolution in England was not attended by near the

EXECUTION OF LOUIS XVI.

suffering that it was in France. England executed her king under process of law; in France the revolution was a mob. But those stormy days have long been past, and the Paris of to-day is not the Paris of the Revolution. In

our next view you see the principal bridge over the Seine, the Pont Neuf.
It is over a third of a mile long and nearly a hundred feet wide. The center
part stands on one of the islands in the Seine. The statue you see is that
of Henry IV. This bridge has more travel than any other bridge in Paris.
By the way, the bronze figure of the horse on which the King is seated had
a little experience of its own. It was cast in Tuscany, sent by ship to
France; but the ship was wrecked off the coast of Normandy, and the horse

THE PONT NEUF.

lay in the bottom of the sea for a year, when it was finally fished up and
carried to its destination."

"But how did they ever find it?" asked Henry.

"I never heard," replied Mr. Adams; "but as the sea is not very deep off
the coast of Normandy, I presume they knew where the vessel sunk, and so
went there and had their divers bring it up."

"I should think it would have been all rusted and spoiled anyway," said
Nettie.

"Oh, as for that, it was bronze, you know; and they could easily clean it up after its year's rest on the bottom of the ocean. At any rate, there it is, seemingly none the worse for its experience.

"Only a few squares from the northern end of Pont Neuf we come to one of those beautiful little public gardens which are scattered over Paris. It is known as the Tour de St. Jacques. The handsome tower you see is

TOUR DE ST. JACQUES.

what is left of a church which once stood on this square. It is 175 feet high, and the view from the top is the finest in Paris. Before us flows the Seine. But a few squares away is the Louvre, the Garden of the Tuileries, the Place de la Concorde, the Champs Elysees; in fact, in all directions we can see objects of interest."

"And if we were there now, I expect we could see the exposition buildings," said Willie.

"Yes, and that famous Eiffel Tower must beat this tower," added Burt, in which opinion Uncle George readily concurred, though he had never seen the Eiffel Tower.

"There are a number of boulevards in Paris; but what is known as the Grand Boulevards are a succession of broad streets extending from the Bastile to the Madeline, forming a rather irregular circular line. Here we have a scene on one of the principal divisions—the Boulevard Montmartre. That gives you a good idea of a street scene in Paris.

BOULEVARD MONTMARTRE.

"How did you say the boulevards were made, uncle?" inquired Willie.

"Why, the boulevards take the places of the old walls. You remember in the view we had of Paris in the seventeenth century, you saw the city walls. The walls of Paris, after being enlarged several times, were finally torn down altogether, and in their place are these boulevards, which are magnificent wide streets. Of late years, however, a number of boulevards have been laid out that had nothing to do with the old city walls."

"I now see why they extend in a kind of circle. They take the same direction as the old walls," added Burt.

"They seem to be having a pretty nice time, anyway. What are they doing—eating?" asked Henry, looking at the picture.

"Yes. Part of the way you can stop most anywhere you want to and partake of refreshments, sit in your easy chairs, smoke cigars, read papers, or, in hot weather, order ices and see the crowd go by."

"There are trees set out along the streets, ain't there?" said Nettie.

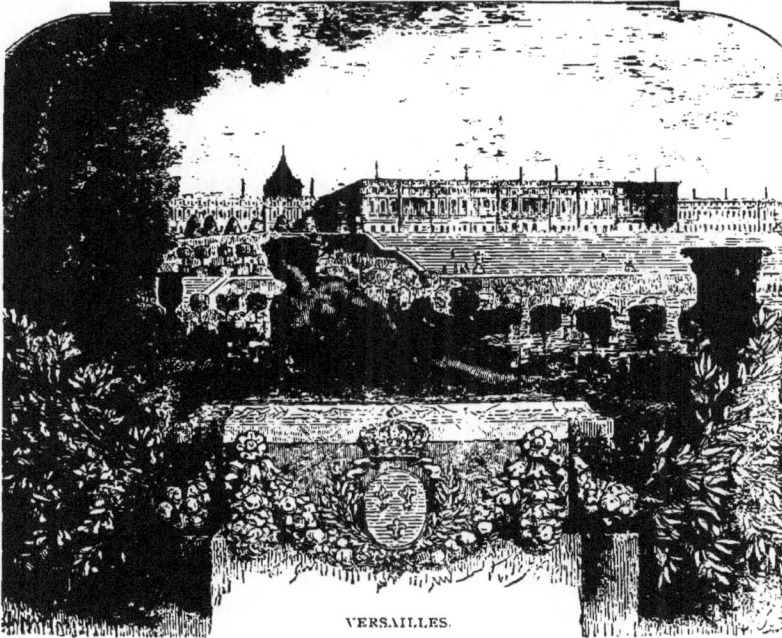

VERSAILLES.

"Yes, and every now and then little gardens, as I have before stated. But we must now turn from the city itself to some of the suburbs. You have all heard more or less of Versailles; this is the one possessing the most interest. It lies twelve miles to the southwest of Paris. Here we have a general view of a portion of the palace. The palace and gardens were constructed by Louis XIV., and of course cost an enormous sum. This made it necessary to increase the taxes, and thus contributed to bringing on the

Revolution. Just think of it, a tract of land sixty miles in circumference
was purchased. The landscape was rendered perfect; hills were leveled or
thrown up; valleys were made or filled as the circumstances demanded;
water was brought from a great distance to supply the lakes and fountains."

THE GRAND TRIANON.

"But how about the grounds, you said they bought for sixty miles
round?" asked Ida.

"Well, here are some views which will give us an idea of how they are
laid out. Notice the labyrinth? The traveler is astonished with the beautiful avenues, the numerous fountains, and the countless groups of statuary,
the flower gardens, lovely lawns, sylvan lakes—well, every imaginable thing
to add to the beauty of the scene."

LABYRINTH OF VERSAILLES.

"And what about that other building—the 'Grand Trianon?'" asked Burt.

"That is a beautiful villa with its grounds, erected by Louis XIV. for Madame Maintenon, who was married to the King in 1686. Of course that building is not to be compared to the palace, but it is exquisitely furnished and adorned, and has interesting historical associations."

NOTRE DAME.

"I would like to see Versailles!" exclaimed Nettie. A sentiment in which we are sure all the club joined.

"Before leaving Paris we must glance at the famous Cathedral of Notre Dame. It stands on the island I have so often mentioned in the Seine. This church has a very beautiful front. Notice the two large square towers, over 200 feet high. The view from the top is very fine, one of the best in Paris. The interior of the church is very beautiful. It was in this church

that Napoleon was crowned as emperor. The traveler in Paris soon discovers what a reverence there is for Napoleon. They remember the glories
of his life-time; they remember how Europe bowed before him when he
commanded the army. I wish I had a view of his tomb, but I see there are
none here. Though he died in St. Helena, his body was brought to Paris,
and rests under the dome of the Hotel des Invalids. But here we have a

ABDICATION OF NAPOLEON.

copy of a celebrated painting of Napoleon. This was when he was in the
full tide of his success. You must read his life some time."

"How long was he emperor, uncle?" asked Willie.

"He was crowned in 1802. He signed his abdication in 1814, and here
is a picture of that event. There is one lesson to be learned from his life.
It shows what can be accomplished by singleness of purpose and a determined
will. In this cut we have represented his abdication, when he gave up his

NAPOLEON I, AS EMPEROR

powers and soon afterward retired to Elba. Of course you all know that
he soon came back, and for a brief space of time resumed his command.
Then came Waterloo and the final defeat, banishment to St. Helena and
death. But now we have been talking a good deal about Paris. We must
take a few trips to other parts of the country. So we will go to that part of
France called Brittany. You will find it in the northwestern part of France.
The people living here belong to the very earliest settlers in France. They
are closely related to the Welsh in Britain—indeed, so closely that I have

PONT AVEN.

heard it said that they could understand each other's language. This is a
very queer part of France, and here we have a view of one of the towns, Pont
Aven. The charm of Brittany is, that the people are so far behind the times
they are almost in the Middle Ages, and they are extremely superstitious.
Here is a place where the people thoroughly believe in witches and fairies,
and have their charms and antidotes. The style of dress—oh, well, everything is exceedingly primitive."

"I shouldn't think that would be a very good place to go to," said Henry.

"It is a great place for artists, Henry. You see there is so much that is quaint, that artists from all over go there to sketch."

"What is that other part of northern France—Normandy?" asked Burt in an inquiring tone.

"Yes; I was just going to speak of Rouen, a city in Normandy. Rouen

STATUE OF JOAN OF ARC.

was the city were dwelt William the Conqueror before he set out on his invasion of England. And he, you know, is quite an important personage in English history. Here we have a view of a famous place or square in Rouen. The statue that you see is that of Joan of Arc; you have all heard more or less of her story."

"But tell me about it, uncle," said Henry, "I haven't heard it."

"Joan of Arc, Henry, was one of those strange characters that you some-times read of. It all happened more than 400 years ago when there was a war between France and England. The French were badly discouraged. Joan of Arc was a simple country girl, pure and innocent, who imagined that she heard voices of angels and spirits urging her to take command of the army and lead the French to victory. It would be too long a story to tell

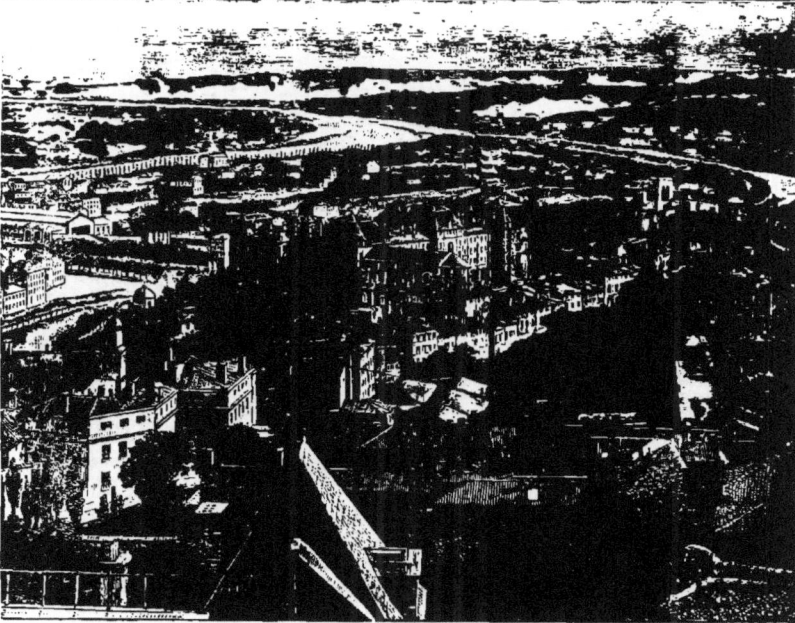

LYONS.

you all about it, but she finally induced the French king to let her lead the army. She was successful, and in less than three months she had accom-plished her purpose. But afterward she was taken prisoner, betrayed into the hands of the English, and was burned in Rouen; the charge against her was that of sorcery. They didn't think she could have done what she did unless she was a witch. Now let us look at some views of a few cities in southern France. Let us take Lyons first. Lyons, you will notice from the

12

map, is at the junction of the Rhone and the Saone. It is the great manufacturing city of France, and the largest city except, of course, Paris. Here
we have a general view of the city. The streets along the rivers are all
embanked and lined with great warehouses. Can any of you tell me what
particular manufactory Lyons is noted for?"

As no one seemed to know, Mr. Adams told them about the silk industry.
It is the greatest center for the manufacturing of silk fabrics in the world.

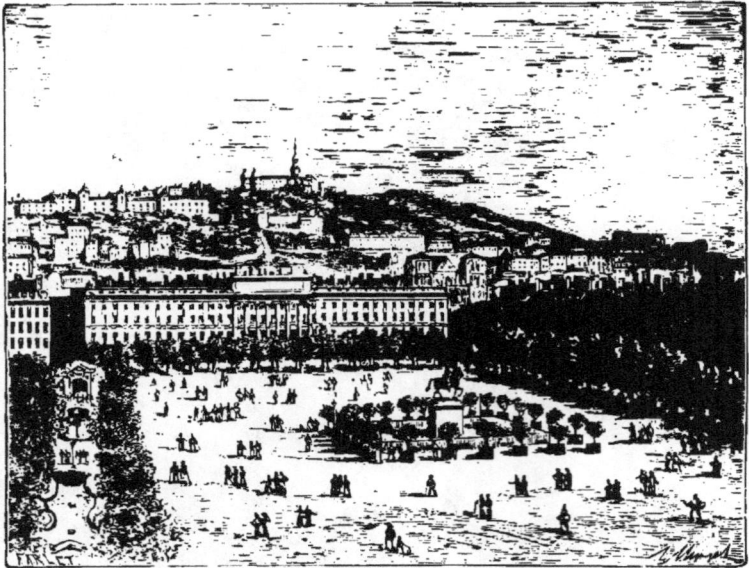

PLACE BELLE COUR.

As they had all seen a Jacquard loom at work in the exposition, they were
much interested to know that Jacquard was a native of Lyons, and that that
invention had revolutionized the manufacture of silk.

"Our next view," continued Uncle George, "is that of one of the public
squares of the city. The people of Lyons claim that this is the most beautiful square in Europe. But the traveler soon recognizes this to be a little
harmless self-conceit, for Paris alone has several squares more beautiful than

that. But, as you see, it is planted with trees, ornamented with basins and fountains, and has two elegant pavilions. This makes it a great place for a promenade, especially when the military band plays."

"Who is that man on horseback?" asked Henry, referring to the statue.

"That is Louis XIV. I was telling you about a little while ago. The first statue put up there of the same king was pulled down in the great Revolutionary times; but a new one, as you see in the picture, was erected in

HOTEL DE VILLE, LYONS.

1825. By the way, when Napoleon was coming back from Elba, he made his first army review in that square. Our next view, I see, is the famous Hotel de Ville. This is one of the nicest buildings in Europe."

"What a nice hotel that must be!" exclaimed Henry.

Uncle George could not repress a laugh as he told him and the club generally that an "Hotel de Ville" was not an hotel as we understand it, but the public municipal building of the city, where all the city business was

attended to. "But for all that," he continued, "it is a very beautiful building. Now, before we leave France, we must glance at rural life. I have
here a little description of a scene in the Valley of the Marne, which Ida may
read. I have not bothered her much with reading this time; and as she
reads it you might glance at this picture of a French village."

Ida read the following description: "As you stroll along, now climb-
ing, now descending this pleasantly undulating country, you may see growing, in less than an acre, a patch of potatoes here, a vineyard there; on one
side a bit of wheat, oats, rye, and barley, with fruit trees casting abundant
shadows over all; further on, a poppy field, three weeks ago in full flower,

GLIMPSE OF A FRENCH VILLAGE.

now having pods ready for gathering; these and many more are found close
together, and near them many a lovely little glen, copse, and ravine, recalling
Scotland and Wales, while the open hill-sides show broad belts of pasture,
corn, and vineyard. You may walk for miles through what seems one vast
orchard—only, instead of turf, rich crops are growing under the trees. This
is, indeed, the orchard of France. Then there are quiet little rivers and
canals winding in between lofty lines of poplars, undulating pastures, and
amber corn-fields; picturesque villages crowned by a church spire here and
there; wide sweeps of highly cultivated land, interspersed with rich woods,
vineyards, orchards, and gardens. We are apt to be struck with the number

of trees to be seen on every side. The banks of the rivers and canals are sure to be lined with poplars. That, however, is the work of the government. Every spare bit of ground belonging to the state is sure to be planted with trees for the sake of the timber. As for the villages, we notice the pains taken to embellish them with shady walks and promenades. The smallest town in the Valley of the Marne has its promenades and avenues for the convenience of the passer-by."

"That is very good," said Uncle George, as she concluded. "Of course not all of France will stand such praise as that; but France is a very rich

CHATEAU OF CHENONCEAUX.

country. There are comparatively few large estates, and there is a great amount of wealth in the country. In this view we have what they call a chateau, a country seat of some wealthy family.

"Traveling in our easy and convenient fashion, we will look at a few views of Spain. To-night we seem to have had a number of historical reminiscences, and so, in the case of Spain, let Henry tell us what Spain had to do with this country."

Henry did not fairly understand what his uncle wanted, but after making it clearer he at once mentioned Columbus.

"That is it exactly," said Uncle George. "We may not find much in

Spain to interest us at present, but we must never forget that once it was a mighty nation and played a great part in the discovery of America; and here we have a view of Columbus at the moment of the discovery of America."

"When we were talking about Norway, uncle, you said something about the Norsemen discovering America. I wish you would tell us something about it," said Burt. "Did Columbus know about it?" he added.

"It is extremely probable that he knew pretty well what he was about," replied Mr. Adams. "It is known that he visited Iceland in 1477, fifteen years before his memorable voyage, and, of course, he must have heard of their expeditions. Still, even earlier than that, he had made known his conviction that by sailing west he could reach land. But it was a most fortunate thing for Spain that America was discovered by her help. You who have read history know how very prosperous Spain was for some centuries. The discovery of America had a great deal to do with that prosperity. It gave the whole nation a start forward. But now let us come back to our trip. Who can tell me the mountains lying between France and Spain?"

This was a very easy question to answer, and they all knew where the Pyrenees were.

"Seeing that question is so easy," continued Uncle George, "I will ask if you know of any country lying between France and Spain?"

"Any country?" exclaimed Willie. "Why, uncle, there ain't any; they come right close together."

"Ah, I thought I would have you there. Didn't any of you ever read of the little republic of Andorra? Well, there it is, at any rate. A little, independent state, with an area of about 200 square miles, and a population not far from 10,000."

"Is it a really true independent country?" asked Ida. "How does it happen that it hasn't been swallowed up by either France or Spain?"

"Yes, indeed, it is a free republic, and has been independent since the days of Charlemagne. The very insignificance of the country and the backward state of the people have tended to keep it free. But national jealousy has done the rest. Neither France nor Spain will permit the other to gobble it up. And now can you tell me of any more interesting people who live in the valleys and defiles of these mountains?"

As none could answer this question, Uncle George told them briefly about the Basques, those strange people who are supposed to represent the primitive inhabitants of Europe.

CARL PILOTY.

COLUMBUS ON THE NIGHT OF OCTOBER 11TH, 1492.   201

"Spain," resumed Uncle George, "is a part of Europe but little visited. You see the scenery is not at all grand. The greater part of it is a stern, melancholy country, with rugged mountains and long, sweeping plains, destitute of trees, and indescribably silent and lonesome. You will not see a country dotted with houses, for the people live in little villages, generally possessing a ruined watch-tower, telling us of past times of insecurity and violence. But, on the other hand, certain elements of the scenery cannot fail

VIEW OF MADRID.

to impress the true traveler. In places are immense plains extending as far as the eye can reach ; in other districts are great mountain chains destitute of shrub or tree, and mottled with variegated marbles and granites. We have been quite a long while on the way, and so if Henry will tell us the capital of Spain, Burt may point it out on the map." But he did not catch Henry this time, and Burt soon pointed out the location of Madrid.

"Here we have a general view of Madrid. It is by no means a beautiful

city, though on a river with an imposing bridge. There is any amount of fun made about the river. It is only a little mountain torrent, and only at certain seasons of the year is it at all imposing. It is not a very old place, as age counts in Europe. But at present it is steadily growing in importance."

"Uncle," suddenly inquired Nettie, "did you ever see a bull fight?"

"Well, yes; I confess I did go to witness one while in Madrid. Of course an old traveler like myself is naturally curious to see all that there is to be seen. But no respectable foreigner cares to see a fight the second time. The best classes of Spaniards are beginning to protest against it. This scene represents the entry of the fighters into an arena.

ENTRY OF THE FIGHTERS INTO THE ARENA.

The great bull ring is capable of seating 14,000 spectators, and once a week it is crowded. But it is a most barbaric spectacle. The men are not in any great danger, although they are pointed out in the streets by admiring people as great heroes. The unfortunate horses are blinded so they cannot see their danger, and they are certain to be killed. The bulls, too, will be killed after they have furnished sufficient sport. It is really surprising how the wealthy and really cultivated inhabitants of Madrid delight to see these exhibitions. The torture is drawn out as long as possible. The miserable horses are patched

LEAPING THE BARRIER.

and made to stand up as long as possible. The bull, after he has killed several horses, is worried by sticking little barbed darts with flags at their end into his neck. Sometimes the base of these darts is filled with powder which explodes when it strikes the bull. It does please a Spanish audience to see the poor animal skip around in his misery. Great dexterity is shown by the men whose duty it is to insert these darts. In this cut you see one of them gracefully leaping the barrier just in time to escape being killed. Here is a description of the final act in the tragedy, which Ida may read."

So Ida read the following: "The matador comes forward, bowing to the audience, and, sword and cap in hand, confronts the bull. It is always an impressive picture. The tortured, maddened animal, whose thin flanks are palpitating with his hot breathings, his coat one shining mass of blood from the darts and spear thrusts, his massive neck still decked as in mockery with the fluttering flags, his fine head and muzzle seeming sharpened by the hour's terrible experience, his formidable horns crimsoned with blood; in front of this fierce bulk of force and courage, the slight, sinewy form of the killer, whose only reliance is on his coolness and intellect. At a favorable moment the sword is thrust to the hilt between the left shoulder and spine, and the bull reels and dies. The heavens are rent with thunderous applause, and in a few minutes another bull bounds into the arena and the barbarous spectacle is again gone through until six bulls have been killed."

"We will now leave Madrid for the southern part of Spain. We will go to Andalusia, and first to the city of Seville. When you get to this part of Spain, we are right in the center of the Moorish or Saracenic Kingdom in Spain. When you read history you will be interested in reading about the Arab conquest of Spain, and the kingdom they established there. Now, what I want especially to call your attention to is some remains of their architecture. Here we have a view of the Alcazar. This word really means a castle. But you must notice the graceful pillars, the high-vaulted hall, the fine stucco work, and, to give us a better idea still, I will show a large view of what is known as the Hall of Embassadors."

THE ALCAZAR.

"Uncle, I want to know a little more about these Moors," said Burt.

"Well, you of course know that when Mohammedanism began to spread, the Arabs had wonderful success wherever they marched. It really seemed

HALL OF AMBASSADORS, SEVILLE.

at one time as if they were going to subdue the world. They crossed over from Northern Africa to Spain. Northern Africa was called by the Romans *Mauritiana*, hence these invaders were called Moors; they were all Mohammedans. They conquered the greater portion of Spain, and for seven centuries held large parts of the peninsula. During that time Spain was one of the most enlightened countries of Europe. It was the home of science during the Dark Ages. Of course they did not rest satisfied with their conquest in Spain, but crossed the Pyrenees and invaded France. Here, how-

DEFEAT OF THE SARACENS BY CHARLES MARTEL.

ever, they were defeated in a terrible battle. And, by the way, we have here a view of that battle, which is one of the most important in history."

"I think they knew how to build real pretty palaces, anyway," said Nettie, still looking at the views of the Alcazar.

"Yes, they undoubtedly did. Ferdinand and Isabella, that helped Columbus discover America, finally drove the Moors out of Spain. But the influence on the country remains to this day. All over Spain you find

scenes reminding you of this era in history. Every little village has its
ruined watch-tower built by the Moors; and, especially in the southern part
of Spain, you continually hear romantic stories about hidden stores of wealth
which the Moors had concealed.   But, talking about the Moors, we must take
a visit to Granada and see the Alhambra."

HALL OF THE TWO SISTERS IN THE ALHAMBRA.

"Oh, yes, uncle!" exclaimed Nettie, "did you go there? I read
Irving's description of that place, and it was ever so nice."

"That is a most charming book.   We could spend a whole evening with
the Alhambra.   Here we have a view of one of the halls known as the ' Hall

216   COURT OF LIONS.

of the Two Sisters.' You must notice how light and graceful the whole scene appears."

"Is the Alhambra another palace?" asked Henry.

"It is far more than a palace. It was an immense fortress, of which the palace formed but a part. In the time of the Moors 40,000 men could be accommodated within the walls of this fortress. It is beautifully situated on an elevated hill overlooking the town of Granada. The Kingdom of Granada was the last stronghold of the Moors, and the Alhambra was their last citadel, where they exerted themselves to the utmost to make a beautiful resort. Here we have another view, the Court of Lions. We will let Ida read this account from Irving's 'Alhambra' which we have here."

Taking the book, Ida read the following: "No part of the edifice gives a more complete idea of its original beauty than this, for none has suffered so little from the ravages of time. In the center stands the fountain, famous in song and story. The alabaster basins still shed their diamond drops; the twelve lions which support them, and give the court its name, still cast forth crystal streams as in the days of Boabdil. Round the four sides of the court are light Arabian arcades of open, filigree work, supported by slender pillars of white marble, which it is supposed were originally gilded. The architecture, like that in most parts of the interior of the palace, is characterized by elegance rather than grandeur, bespeaking a delicate and graceful taste and a disposition to indolent enjoyment. When one looks upon the fairy traces of the peristyles, and the apparently fragile fretwork of the walls, it is difficult to believe that so much has survived the wear and tear of centuries, the shocks of earthquakes, the violence of war, and the quiet though less baneful pilferings of the tasteful traveler."

"That is very good," said Uncle George, "and now I want to say in general that when you first glance at these pictures you are apt to think that it is exquisite carving in stone, but, in fact, the wall ornamentation is stucco or plaster of Paris work; but for all that the effect is very pretty. Now we have no further time this evening, but I might remark that in the cathedral at Granada is the tomb of Ferdinand and Isabella. Now I think we have gone far enough for to-night. I only wish we could take more time and travel more slowly, but this way gives us a pretty good idea of a country after all."

Then ensued the usual desultory conversation and explanations, which

13

need not concern us.   The next trip was announced as a trip to classical Italy. We can safely say that the club indulged in lively anticipations of an enjoyable time when they should meet again.   They had now been over a considerable part of Europe; had been hearing a great deal about the ancient Romans, and they were glad of a chance to clear up their rather vague thoughts about that people.

TOMB OF FERDINAND AND ISABELLA.

CHAPTER VI.

ITALY.

WE ARE to visit Italy to-night, children," began Uncle George, when the club had assembled for the fifth meeting, and in that sunny land we have a good deal more to do than simply to see what is to be seen at the present day. This is the historic land, and in order to enjoy our visit we must talk a good deal of history. But this will make the evening much more instructive and enjoyable to us. You know all along in our trip so far we have been talking about Roman days and Roman times. Well, we have now reached the very home of the Romans. We shall see a good many ruins of their greatness, and I think we can not do better than to talk a good deal about the old Romans. So, Burt, you get the atlas open at the right place, Italy, so that we may keep the geography straight, and we will talk history for a little while."

There was no objection to this program. Henry was satisfied, provided he had some pictures to look at and some stories to hear.

CAPITOLINE WOLF.

"You all know," continued Uncle George, "in a general way, about the great Roman Empire. We have every evidence that for a long series of years that power, which was afterwards called Rome, was slowly growing on the banks of the Tiber. Historic light in the case of Rome only goes back to the end of the third century B. C.; back of that time we have a most confused stock of legendary stories—nice enough stories, but of no value as far as history is concerned. We have interesting stories about the famous twins, Romulus and Remus, who were nourished by the wolf represented in this bit of old sculpture shown here."

"Do you say there is nothing in that story, uncle?" asked Willie.

"Oh, no; that story is what we call a myth. There has been a wonderful

collection of such stories in the case of Roman history. Some of them may
be true, but we know nothing definitely about them. But we do know that,
at the time of the birth of Christ, Rome was the one great power in the
world. The Mediterranean was simply a Roman lake. On all sides of it

IMPERIAL ROME.

were provinces of
this mighty em-
pire; and so we
want to ask a
good deal about
the old Romans
themselves. We
have here a view
of Rome at the
time of her great-
est power. Of
course, this is a
fanciful s c e n e;
and yet it prob-

ably possesses
many elements
of truth."

"What funny
looking boats!"
exclaimed Hen-
ry.

"They do look
rather strange
to us, don't they?
As you are some-
what interested
in that, I will
show you this

ANCIENT ROMAN SHIP.

view of an old Roman ship, so you can see what they are when you get near
to them. The Romans used to take great long voyages in such ships as
that; they sailed the Mediterranean in all directions, and, as you know,
Cæsar crossed the English Channel and invaded England by means of such

boats. But, coming back to the first picture, the grand houses you see are public buildings and temples. The regular private houses of the citizens were one-storied buildings, having three or four large halls opening into each other. Here is a view of an

A ROMAN VILLA.

ENTRANCE TO A ROMAN HOUSE.

entrance to such a house, together with a view of a villa of a rich Roman."

"What is that word 'salve' at the opening?" asked Burt, pointing to the picture.

"That is like our word 'welcome.' It was their method of greeting a visitor," explained Uncle George. "In the immediate suburbs were the beautiful villas of the rich—such as the villa of Seneca on the Appian Way, only four miles from Rome."

"That villa, as you call it, has more than one story," said Ida.

"Yes. Well, in the city there were large tenement houses that were several stories in height. I might add that the private houses had no opening for light facing the street, so they looked more like castles than houses."

"That villa wouldn't be a bad place to live in now," said Willie."

"No, indeed. They were fitted up with every luxury that that age could command; and yet they lacked many of our every day comforts. We would think it pretty difficult to fix up a comfortable house without glass, wouldn't we? And so of a great many other things. But they managed to enjoy

ROMAN LADY AT HER TOILET.

themselves. In this picture of a Roman lady at her toilet, you see her waited on by her slaves, and articles of luxury scattered around the room."

"Slaves!" exclaimed Willie. "Why, they look as white as any of the others."

"But, for all that, they were slaves. The Romans were great slave-holders. In the latter days of the republic it is estimated that two-thirds of the people in Rome were slaves. You see, the captives taken in the wars were sold into slavery. Wealthy men used to follow up the armies and buy the slaves after a successful battle."

"Were they cruel to them—I mean the owners?" asked Nettie.

"Well, yes; they were. But, of course, there was a difference between their lot and that of the slaves we used to have in this country. They were often set free and could become honored citizens. But, as a general thing, their lot could not have been particularly a happy one. Some rich Romans had a vast number of slaves. They used them for every conceivable purpose.

WALL ORNAMENT AT POMPEII.

From the moment a stranger entered the house, his every want was attended to by slaves; different slaves for each purpose."

"There seems to be a good many plants in the room," said Ida, pointing them out in the picture.

"Oh, yes; in all ages of the world people have delighted in flowers. You furthermore notice that the walls are ornamented, and there is a statue. Here we have a nearer view of such ornamented walls. This was found at Pompeii, of which place we will speak soon."

"What is that supposed to be in that black space—an angel?" asked Willie.

"They probably didn't call it an angel, and, for that matter, knew nothing about what we believe in as angels. But then every people believed in good and evil spirits, good genii, etc., and that prob-

FURNITURE ETC., IN THE ROOM OF A RICH ROMAN.

ably represents some such a conception. Look sharp and you will see some more little kneeling figures there. So you see the Romans tried to make their homes as cheerful as they knew how with what they had to work with. At the present we have learned how to enjoy life, so that the poorest has more real enjoyment now than the richest then."

"Did they have furniture in their rooms, the way we have?" asked Ida.

"Of course their rooms were furnished, but not as ours are—you would have found no Brussels carpets or large mirrors. Here we have a view of the furniture in the room of a rich Roman. On the table you see books that are rolls of manu-

HOUSEHOLD UTENSILS.

script; musical instruments on the floor, lamps, etc., and the conch with its coverings. The various implements, of course, speak for themselves. Some of them look quite natural, don't they?"

"What did you say about their books, uncle?" inquired Burt.

"Why, you know they had no printing in those days; the only way in which books could be multiplied was by copying the contents, and they used great rolls of papyrus for this purpose. We would think that a pretty slow way of increasing the copies of a book. Often slaves were trained for this purpose."

"I shouldn't think any one would read them when they were made," said Ida.

"Of course, there was not near the amount of reading done then as at present," replied Mr. Adams. "It is hard to see how the world could have made very great progress if some one had not hit on the invention of printing," he added after a brief pause. "The dining room of a Roman house," resumed Uncle George, "was sometimes fitted up with great elegance. Nero had one in his palace built something like a theater, with shifting scenes that could change with each course. Here we have a dining room."

ROMAN DINING HALL.

"But where are the tables and chairs?" asked Nettie.

"They reclined on the couches you see here—resting on the left elbow, supported by cushions. There were usually three on the same couch, the middle place being the place of honor."

"I believe I had rather sit up at the table," said Henry. How did they use their knives and forks?"

"Why, they didn't have them, Henry; they used their fingers. When the guests dressed for a dinner, they usually put on some bright colored robe variegated with flowers. They took off their shoes for fear of soiling the couch, which was often inlaid with ivory or tortoise shell and covered with a cloth of gold. The servants were arranged around the table much as at present."

"I suppose they had about the same things to eat that we do?" inquired Willie.

"Well, yes; on the whole. They ate some things we don't—such as peacocks; and they lacked some things we have—such as potatoes; but

A ROMAN CITIZEN.   A ROMAN MATRON.

they had a plentiful supply of meat and vegetables. But now a word about the people who lived in these houses. We have here a picture of a Roman citizen and matron."

"But how funny the man is dressed," said Nettie with a laugh. "What is that funny thing he has on?"

"That," said Uncle George with a smile, "is a toga; the garment the lady is represented as wearing is a tunica. The toga was the great garment among the Romans. They had them made of different materials, or colored differently, according to the rank of the citizen—a purple toga always being a sign of high office, and in the latter days was worn by the emperors. And so you see the meaning of the old saying, when speaking of some fortunate individual, that 'he was born to the purple.' A white toga with a purple border was worn by those holding a public office, by the priests, and by boys up to the sixteenth year. We would hardly expect it, but the Romans were very fond of wearing rings; they often had one on each finger. Many persons possessed great collections of them, and the ladies, too, were quite up to some modern people in the way of heightening their charms. They knew how to dye the hair, to paint and powder. When boys reached the

FUNERAL CEREMONIES.

adult stage, they put off the white toga with a purple border, and donned the toga virilis. Such occasions were very formal, ceremonious affairs. Now, as we are interested in all the particulars of the lives of the Romans, I have here some views of their funeral ceremonies. In the first we see the body lying in state surrounded by friends. You notice the censer burning at the side, and there are the musicians playing their wailing dirges."

"Some of the folks feel pretty bad, I guess," said Henry.

"Ah, yes; it makes no difference whether they were Romans or any one else, death always fills the heart with sorrow. Parting is always sad, whether the beloved one be a little child that we have learned to love, or whether some aged one whose time of departure could not be long delayed; our hearts ache when death approaches. But in our next picture you see a custom that seems strange to us. This is the place of eating the funeral meal nine days after death. It was regarded as a sort of farewell meal. Only simple dishes were partaken of near the grave. But sometimes games were provided for the general multitude, who were likewise regaled with goods and presents of money."

"That was something like a wake that we read of now and then, ain't it, uncle?" asked Willie.

"Yes; there is probably some sort of connection between them, but a great many people have had nearly the same sort of customs."

PLACE OF EATING THE FUNERAL MEAL.

"What are they doing in that next picture?" asked Henry, who evidently wanted to hurry the thing along.

"The custom was, in the case of distinguished men, for one of his friends to pronounce a funeral oration over the remains. The most celebrated one is probably the oration of Anthony over Cæsar, of which we have a fine view. But, after all, we don't know much about that, only what Shakespeare imagines him to say."

"The people seem to be getting mad, anyway," said Henry, still looking at the picture.

"I wonder, did they believe the way we do about death?" inquired Ida.

MARC ANTHONY DELIVERS THE FUNERAL ORATION OVER THE DEAD BODY OF JULIUS CÆSAR.

225

"Now that introduces us to another subject I wanted to speak about. Of course they knew nothing about Christianity; but then, you know, all people have some sort of religion, and in general they have hoped for a life beyond the grave. They worshipped their household gods—that is, the spirits of their ancestors. The sad feature about the heathen religions was that they did not satisfy the intellect, and so as the people advanced in culture they became skeptical and refused to believe in anything. That was the case in

OFFERINGS OF THE VESTAL VIRGINS.

cultured and wealthy Rome at the time of Christ. The higher classes had lost all interest in religion, though they still upheld the state religion as a matter of policy. We have views, as you see, of the Vestal Virgins attending to their duties. The Vestal Virgins, I might remark, were maidens vowed to a life of celibacy; their principal duty was to guard the sacred fire, representative of the goddess Vesta. They were greatly respected by the Romans. The lower classes were, of course, as superstitious as ever. But among the middle classes there was growing the knowledge of semi-mystical religion, like the worship of Serapis. But I must be careful, or I will be talking about things you don't understand."

"Why, no, uncle; I am sure we all like to hear about that, and here is another curious picture—what about that?" said Burt, pointing to the open book of views.

"Well, I will explain about that," said Uncle George. "That is a Roman Haruspex. You see, the Romans were very superstitious and believed in witchcraft and sorcery, and had their priests who believed they could foretell future events by the appearance of slaughtered fowls. That was a funny idea, wasn't it? But people never reason when it comes to superstitious customs. The Romans most devoutly believed in this custom. They never would undertake any important movement unless the augurs assured them the time was propitious. Armies were not marched, important battles were delayed until all those skilled in this method of fortune-telling had decided that all was ready. Now we must talk about the public life of the old Romans. Just before the Christian era, Rome changed from a republic to an empire; and here we have a view of the first emperor, Augustus, and his intimate companions. It was during his reign that Jesus Christ was born in the Roman province of Judea.

"In our next view we have represented a Roman judgment hall, or

COURT OF AUGUSTUS.

A ROMAN HARUSPEX.

Court of Justice. You probably do not know it, but the fact is, the greatest influence the Romans have exerted on the civilization of to-day has been in the field of law. In the city of Florence is a copy of the 'digests' of Roman law, made by order of Justinian, which is considered of very great value. It is kept under a glass cover constantly guarded, nobody being permitted to touch it unless by special permission. In fact, so great is the value attributed

ROMAN JUDGMENT HALL.

to this manuscript, that a formal ceremony is enacted while the spectators gaze on it. Among others, servants with torches in hand, and soldiers with drawn swords, stand round during the examination."

"That is a funny way to do," remarked Nettie.

"Yes, it is; and there is not much sense about it now. But I suppose it is a relic of an old custom, and I have more than once told you that when a

I.1

custom gets started in Europe, it is a very difficult matter to break it up.
Of course, Rome was the great military power of the world. They had
arisen to power by means of war, so the god of war was a very important
god among them. Before their soldiers left on distant expeditions, an offering was made to him, as is shown here."

"They generally came out ahead in their wars, I suppose," said Burt.

"For a long while they did. But now and then they used to get
whipped. It was during the reign of Augustus that three legions of Roman
soldiers, under the command of Varus, were completely destroyed in battle
with the partially civilized Germans. But for a number of centuries Rome

OFFERINGS TO MARS.

carried everything before her; and when her successful generals would come
back from a glorious campaign, the Senate would decree them what they
called a triumph."

"What was a triumph?" asked Henry.

"Why, a great procession would be formed of the victorious army. If
they had taken important captives, they would be sometimes led along
chained to the chariot of the conquering general. Everything was done to
make the scene one long to be remembered. Now, perhaps, the best thing
we can do is to take a little trip in Rome, and talk about some of the ruins
and the history that belongs to them. If we were in the city of Rome to-day,
we would want to walk down the Corso, the principal street in Rome, running

THE ROMAN FORUM.

234

south from the Piazza Del Popolo. We would pass innumerable objects of interest. Finally we come to the very center of the old city, to the Forum. This was a level plat of ground between the Capitoline and Palatine hills. We have a full page view of this most interesting spot."

"What is there about it so interesting, uncle?" inquired Willie.

"Why, it was the heart of the Roman Empire, where its public business was transacted, where great questions of policy were discussed. So it became crowded with marble temples, state buildings, and courts of law to such an extent that we wonder how there was room for them all within such a narrow area. There were monuments of great men, statues of Greek sculpture,

THE FORUM.

colonnades and porticoes, rich with the spoil of subject kingdoms. I have here a smaller view of a part of the Forum as it must have looked when it was surrounded on all sides by public buildings. Notice the pillars and statues; that figure on horseback, by the way, still exists, and is a beautiful work of art. It is the statue of a noted emperor, Marcus Aurelius. The general direction of the Forum is from north to south, and every part of it is historic ground. For instance, in the large picture in the background, close by the arch, you see a building with a tower on it; the lower part of that building is the old capitol of Rome. I have another view of that building, giving us a probable idea of the scene to be observed before it once."

"What a funny kind of a cart that is," said Henry.

"Yes; that is their chariot. I guess we would not think it much of a chariot, would we? Not having any springs, it would seem to us about as comfortable as a lumber wagon. Beneath the building were the treasury vaults of Rome, excavated in the solid rock on which the building stood; and as the army was paid in coppers, most spacious vaults had to be employed. The second story of the old capitol is now employed as a museum, where the most interesting and valuable finds—that are always being made—

ENTRANCE TO THE CAPITOL.

are exhibited. The most interesting buildings of ancient Rome stood in the Forum. There are yet to be seen the remains of the Royal Palace, the residence of the Pontifex Maximus, or high priest. Julius Cæsar lived there during the greater part of his life. Afterward it became the home of the Vestal Virgins—you know we just looked at some pictures of them. The Temple of Vesta stood near by. In this view we have a picture of a famous temple which stood on the Capitoline Hill; this was the Temple of Jupiter.

The story has it that this temple was built by the mythical Romulus, but it probably was built by the Etruscans, who probably lived here long before the Romans arrived on the scene. This was a most splendid building. Triumphal processions of Roman soldiers marched up to this temple when they returned victorious from their wars, carrying with them the spoils of their campaigns. It was in this temple that Cicero made his first oration against Cataline. I have not begun to mention all the interesting remains to

FACADE OF JUPITER STATOR'S TEMPLE.

be seen in the Forum. And probably before many years the government will have completed its excavation."

"Excavation!" exclaimed Burt. Why, how did it get buried up?"

"Why, yes; the entire Forum was covered with from fifteen to twenty feet of soil. And for a number of years excavations have been in progress, and still a most interesting part of it is buried beneath the rubbish of many centuries. The trouble is, that valuable buildings are erected on that portion, which of course would have to be removed before the work can proceed. Starting at the Forum was the celebrated Appian Way. I can not recall a

walk more interesting to the historian than a stroll along this ruined highway. The Romans were celebrated for making good roads—the Appian Way
was the most celebrated of these roads. It led from Rome to Brindisi on the
Adriatic, and was thus the great highway for travelers from Greece and the
East generally to Rome. It was paved throughout with broad, six-sided
slabs of lava exactly fitted to each other; it was twenty-six feet in width from
curb to curb; every forty feet were placed low columns as seats on which to
rest or to assist the horseman in mounting; every five thousand feet were
placed milestones—they were circular shafts with pedestals and appropriate
inscriptions. Inns were scattered along the route, and statues of the various

THE APPIAN WAY.

gods and goddesses enlivened the scene. In the palmy days of ancient
Rome, the first fifteen miles of way, or from Rome to the blue Alban Hills,
was almost one continuous suburb. It was adorned with all the charms of
nature and art, palatial villas and pleasure gardens, groves and vineyards,
temples and aqueducts. Crowds of chariots and horsemen and wayfarers
thronged the road from morning to night. In recent years they have laid
bare that part of the road from the third to the eleventh milestone, so that
you can now see the very pavement along which the old Roman emperors
and generals frequently passed; and once, at least, Paul. The view we have
given shows us the nature of the scene."

" Did you mean the Apostle Paul walked along that road?" asked Nettie.

" Why, yes. You know we read in the Acts of Paul going a prisoner to Rome. The direct route from Puteoli to Rome was along this road. We can only imagine with what varied emotions he must have approached the city, then a magnificent metropolis of nearly 2,000,000 inhabitants. Rather opposed to our ideas of propriety, the Romans placed on the sides of the roads entering the city the tombs of patrician families; and, as we might suppose, the Appian Way was especially distinguished by the number and magnificence of its tombs. Some of the most illustrious people of ancient

TOMB OF CÆCILIA METALLA.

Rome were buried here, and their monuments were of great beauty and elegance. Some of them were fashioned as conical mounds, on the slopes of which trees and parterres of flowers were planted; others were built after the models of graceful Grecian temples; others were huge circular masses of masonry; still others were simple sarcophagi, with lids resting on square elevated pedestals; many of them were adorned with busts and statues of the departed, with altars, columns, and carvings. What these tombs were in their prime, it is difficult for us to imagine. I have here a view of one of the most celebrated of these tombs—that of Cæcilia Metalla, wife of the millionaire, Crœsus. The appearance of this tower in the afternoon sun is very striking. It is built on a portion of rising ground, the roadway being sunk several feet below the general level, so as to make the grade as light as possible. The sort of battlement on top is a modern addition; the tomb itself has a massive conical roof. Now, here is a verse of poetry that Lord Byron wrote of this tomb, which Ida may read."

So Ida read from "Childe Harold:"

> There is a stern round tower of other days,
>   Firm as a fortress, with its fence of stone,
> Such as an army's baffled strength delays,
>   Standing with half its battlements alone,
>   And with two thousand years of ivy grown,
> The garland of eternity, where wave
>   The green leaves o'er it all by time o'erthrown.
> What was this tower of strength? Within its cave
> What treasure lay so locked, so hid? A woman's grave.

"Just think a moment," said Uncle George as Ida ceased reading, "of the wonderful changes the country has witnessed since that tomb received its occupant. The great empire of Rome, which then seemed so strong, long since passed away; Europe has become civilized, and a new world has been discovered and settled. I have here a beautiful extract from a late work about the Appian Way, which Willie may read."

Willie read the following extract: "On every side are innumerable tokens of a vast expenditure of human toil, and love, and sorrow; and it seems as if it had been all thrown away. For two miles and a half from the tomb of Cæcilia Metalla I counted fifty-three tombs on the right, and forty-eight on the left. Broken tablets, retaining a few letters of the epitaphs of the dead; mutilated statues and alto-relievos; drums and capitals of pillars; a hand or a foot, or a fold of marble drapery; every form and variety of sculpture. The mere crumbs that had fallen from a profuse feast of artistic beauty, which nobody considers it worth while to pick up, lie moldering among the grass. At frequent intervals facing the road you see with mournful interest the exposed interiors of tombs robbed of their treasures. Pitying hands have lately endeavored to atone for this desecration by lifting here and there out of the rubbish heap on which they were thrown some affecting group of family portraits, some choice specimens of delicate architecture,

SCENE IN THE CATACOMBS.

some mutilated panel, on which the stern, hard features of a Roman Senator look out upon you, and placing them in a prominent position to attract attention."

"I would think that would be rather of a sad walk," remarked Nettie, thoughtfully.

"Well, it is sad," replied Uncle George; "or, perhaps, we had better say that it calls up mournful reflections in the mind of any thoughtful person. But, talking about the tombs, I might remark that some of the most extensive catacombs of Rome are alongside of the Appian Way, and here we have a view of a fanciful scene, probably not far from the truth, of an occurrence that took place many centuries ago."

"But what are they doing, and what is a catacomb?" queried Henry.

"A catacomb, Henry, was a place where long passage ways were dug in solid rock, like a coal mine, with

COLOSSEUM AT ROME.

branches running in all directions, and then niches dug out and coffins were put in them on the sides. In the early centuries of our era the Christians buried most of their dead in catacombs, and this picture is supposed to represent the relatives visiting the place where some loved member of the family rests. But we must hurry along, so we will go back to our starting point, that is the Forum. Let me see," resumed Uncle George thoughtfully, "probably the Colosseum would be the first ruin to catch the eye as we continued on our stroll, and here we have a view of it. The Colosseum was simply an immense amphitheater where public games of all kinds, of which the Romans were very fond, were publicly exhibited.

This was an enormous building. When entire it was 157 feet high and nearly 2,000 feet in circumference. Like many other famous monuments of antiquity it is disappointing at first sight, but grows in impressiveness the longer it is viewed. It was so large that nearly 100,000 spectators could be comfortably accommodated with seats and witness the combat of several hundred men and animals in the immense arena. The wealth and luxury of Rome were used to her utmost to adorn it. Portions of it were encrusted

GLADIATORIAL GAMES.

with costly marbles; network of gilt bronze, supported by stakes and wheels of ivory, guarded the people from the beasts; the spaces between the seats glittered with gold and gems; a portico carried around the entire building was resplendent with gilded columns; marble statues thronged the arcades; the awnings were of silk; marble tripods for burning perfumes were placed here and there, and costly fountains bubbled forth with perfumed waters. And here were held the gladiatorial games as shown in this cut. The gladiators were regularly trained for their art. They were largely slaves, criminals, prisoners of war, and in latter days Christians."

"Spartacus was a gladiator, wasn't he?" exclaimed Nettie. "You know we had to read his speech to-day for our reading lesson. How the teacher did make us ring that out: 'If we must fight, let us fight for ourselves; if we must slaughter, let us slaughter our oppressors; if we must die, let us die under the open sky, by the bright waters, in noble, honorable battle!'"

ARCH OF CONSTANTINE.

Uncle George could not help laughing as Nettie recited this little extract, and then he told them about Spartacus, the gladiator.

"Right near the Colosseum is a most interesting arch which I have represented in this view—the Arch of Constantine. Constantine was the first Christian emperor, though it must be confessed that he was not a very good example of a Christian. Although the arch is dedicated to Constantine, yet it was an old arch to Isis, decorated by reliefs taken from the Arch of Trajan, and only a small part of it was new and appropriate to Constantine."

"I shouldn't think he would want such an arch as that," said Burt.

"I don't think it showed very good taste, myself," continued Uncle George, "but Constantine was a strange character, and owes most of his fame to the fact that the new religion, Christianity, got the upper hand of heathenism in his reign. But we must pass along. But a few squares to the southwest of the Colosseum we come to a ruin of which but few traces now remain, but which was once of great renown. This brings us to the Circus Maximus, and I see we have a view of it. This great circus has almost entirely disappeared, though some traces of it may be seen under the walls of some houses in the Via de Cerchi."

CIRCUS MAXIMUS.

"And what did they have in their circus?" asked Henry. "What we have in ours?" he continued.

"Oh, all sorts

CHARIOT RACE.

of athletic contests, games, and chariot races. This last was a very favorite diversion with the Romans. You see we have a view of a chariot race. They enjoyed this kind of a race fully as much as people nowadays do our races. Lists of the horses with their names and colors and those of the drivers were handed about, and heavy bets made upon each faction; and some-

times the contests between two parties broke out into open violence and bloody quarrels. One of the late emperors, Justinian, nearly lost his crown in consequence of disputes which originated in the circus. Now," resumed Uncle George, "perhaps we had better examine some of the views to be seen in Rome at the present time. As you know, Rome is the headquarters of the Catholic Church, so, of course, we want to visit that part of the city where

BRIDGE OF ST. ANGELO.

the Vatican is. So starting once more from the Piazza del Popolo we come to the bridge of St. Angelo, and here is a view of it. You see it adorned with statues."

"And what about the big building that it leads to?" asked Willie.

"That is now known as the Castle of St. Angelo, but in the first place it was the mausoleum of the Emperor Hadrian. It was built early in the

15

second century, and was a really magnificent building; it was covered with white marble, and decorated with statues of gods and heroes.   After serving

ST. PETER'S CATHEDRAL.

as a tomb for Hadrian for about four centuries it was turned into a fortress. We now come to one of the wonders of Rome, the long-wished-for goal of many pious pilgrims, the celebrated Cathedral of St. Peter — the largest church in the world. First I will show you a view of the approach to the cathedral. The open space in front includes about ten acres; it is paved with square blocks of lava crossed by marble walks, and in the center is an immense Egyptian obelisk. Notice the fine fountains on the sides, and especially the two great semi-circular colonnades. You see there are four rows of columns, each column being forty-two feet and a half in height; and, looking at the balustrade along the top, you see a long row of statues; each is sixteen feet in height. I guess you will agree that that is a most magnificent approach to a church."

"And how long was that church building, as long as that cathedral at Cologne?" asked Henry.

"Not quite as long," responded Uncle George. It was building during a period of 175 years, but, of course, workmen were not employed on it all that time. Some fifteen different architects had charge of the building. The most celebrated one, by the way, was Michael Angelo, and I see I have a small cut of him here. He was a most remarkable man. In many different ways he was renowned as an artist. There was a church standing on the site of St. Peter's from very early times, built, it is said, to commemorate the place where St. Peter suffered mar-

MICHAEL ANGELO.

tyrdom. Then they finally resolved to build a church which should surpass all others. When Michael Angelo took charge of the work as architect, he was in his seventy-second year; but, being dissatisfied with the existing plans, shut himself up in his room, and in fifteen days made an entirely new plan. He did not live to see them completed, but, on the whole, they have been carried out; and wherever they were changed it is now acknowledged that it was a mistake to do so."

"And how big is the church itself?" asked Willie.

"Figures alone do not give us a very good idea. The actual amount of space covered by the church exceeds an acre and a half; there are more than 450 columns within and without the building, and there are nearly 400 statues. The cross you see on the top of the dome is 453 feet from the ground. As this is such an important church," continued Mr. Adams, "I will show you this view of the interior; but, of course, this will not begin to give you a true idea of the grandeur of the scene."

"What do they do in such a fine church?" asked Henry.

INTERIOR OF ST. PETER'S AT ROME.

"Well, the great ceremonies of the church are held there. There the new Pope is crowned; and at Christmas, Easter, and the festival of St. Peter's and St. Paul, the Pope celebrates mass there in person; and then on **Palm** Sunday he blesses the palms, and so on other great church occasions **the** cathedral is used. Previous to the year 1870 one of the very finest sights to be seen in Rome was the illumination of St. Peter's at Easter. Four hundred men were stationed at various places within and without the church, and at

a given signal lamps were lit all over the church. In less than a minute the
building would be one blaze of light; and, of course, owing to the vast size
of the building, the effect was very grand. There are, besides, many interesting things to see within the church. There are, for instance, no less than
forty-six altars and 121 lamps, the greater number of which are always kept
burning. In one place there is a famous bronze statue of St. Peter, of which
pilgrims have been accustomed to kiss the great toe; it has actually been
worn out of shape by the kisses of the faithful. One hundred and thirty-two
popes have been buried in this church. Adjoining it is the Vatican—the
palace of the popes. We could spend the whole evening talking about the
interesting sights to be seen in the Vatican. There is the famous Sixtine
Chapel, the walls and ceilings are covered by the most magnificent series of
frescoes the world has ever seen; then there are a series of rooms decorated
by the great artist, Raphael; in the picture gallery are some of the most
famous paintings in the world; the collection of sculpture is also very fine;
in the library are over 24,000 valuable manuscripts, and a much larger
number of valuable books. One of the MSS., by the way, is an extremely
early copy of the New Testament, and, on that account, very valuable. Now
we must glance at some of the other cities of Italy, though we have not
begun to exhaust the sights of Rome."

"One question if you please, uncle!" exclaimed Burt. "Why is Rome
called the Eternal City; is it because it is so very old?"

"No, not that; it is not as old as Athens, for instance. But it has been
a very important city since the third century before Christ. It was the
capital of the great Roman Empire. Then, when the Catholic Church
became firmly established, it was the capital, so to speak, of that church.
The official residence of the Pope is there, and thus it is the center of ecclesi-
astical authority for that important denomination."

The club was not particularly anxious to have Uncle George hurry on,
but when he mentioned Venice they were reconciled to the change, since they
had heard considerable of that place.

"Venice," continued Uncle George, "is an interesting place to visit;
and it, too, is interesting from its historical reminiscences. A few centuries
ago it was rich and powerful, but now it is but a shadow of its former self.
It is built on over 100 small islands, situated in an extensive lagoon in the
Gulf of Venice. It is difficult to get at, but a railroad bridge about two

miles long leads from the main land to the principal island.   What they call
the Grand Canal takes a winding course through the city.   This water-way

THE GRAND CANAL, VENICE.

is broad and deep, and in general is lined with fine buildings like that one
shown in this view.   That is the Church of St. Mark's in the distance."

"Ain't there any streets in Venice, where horses and carriages can go on?" asked Henry.

"There are no streets for horses, Henry; but then nearly every canal, big and little, has foot-walks bordering it and bridges crossing it, so that you can go all over the city if you want to on foot. There are only three bridges, however, crossing the Grand Canal. And, by the way, I have here a view of the Rialto; that is a famous bridge, and the oldest one crossing the Grand Canal. But, owing to the numerous canals, the principal means of getting

GONDOLA.

around is by means of gondolas—of course you have all heard of them. I have a small view of one."

"I saw one at the exposition in Cincinnati last year when I went there with papa," broke in Henry.

"Sure enough," said Uncle George,

THE RIALTO AT VENICE.

"I read they had some there. Well, as you have seen them, I do not need to talk longer about them. But in Venice they take the place of cabs and street cars. Now, arrived in the city, one of the principal sights is a visit to the Square of St. Mark's—or the Piazza of St. Mark's, as it is called there. It is not a very large square, but it is one of the grandest in Europe. This is the heart of the city, and in older times it was connected with all of the great events in the history of the republic. The building we see before us is the famous Cathedral of St. Mark's. That is a most magnificent building and splendidly decorated. In the Middle Ages every Venetian galley trading

PIAZZA OF ST. MARK'S.

to the East was expected to bring back some trophy to ornament the church. It fills nearly the whole of one side of the square, and the traveler is fairly bewildered at the imposing display. Passing within the church, the scene is extremely beautiful. Fragments of colored glass, imbedded in a ground-work of gold, are so arranged as to form figures and landscapes, groups and individuals; there are gorgeous altars, marble pillars, cornices, and sculp-tured saints. In short, you are viewing the church that the richest and most

THE DUCAL PALACE, VENICE.

powerful city in Europe strove in every way to render attractive, and she succeeded."

" It is no wonder they call that a nice square " said Ida, with enthusiasm.

" No, indeed; this is only one of the fine buildings. On the right, adjoining this church, is the famous Ducal Palace of Venice, the seat of government, where the Doges held office. The Doge, as you know, was the chief executive of Venice. The interest of this building is chiefly historical, and it gives us no bad idea of the ancient government. You see how the front is ornamented with foliage, figures, and symbols; within, the walls are decorated by frescoes and paintings. In one room there are paintings of many of the old Doges. The paintings which cover many of the walls are of great historical interest; many of them represent events which had a great deal to do with the history of the Middle Ages."

"I have read a good deal about the Doge of Venice," said Burt.

"I dare say," replied Uncle George, "he was quite an important personage of the Middle Ages. For a century or over he was almost absolute; he made war or peace, commanded the army and navy, and, in short, his will was law. But they found a way to cut short his powers. By his oath of office, he promised to keep secret affairs of state, to read no letters from abroad except when his councilors were present, to send no dispatches, to give audience to no embassadors, to return no response to any demand, to receive no gifts, to possess no property without the limits of the republic, to erect or repair no monuments, never to leave Venice without permission, never to receive in private generals of the republic, and not to permit any member of his family to hold any office, either within or without Venice. All these promises were renewed once every month. We need not wonder, then, that the office was very little sought after. In short, he was a figure-head for the council.

"I don't think he had a very good time in that nice palace," said Henry.

"Those in power are often to be pitied rather than envied," replied Uncle George. "But we must pass on. Lord Bryon has some beautiful verses on Venice. Let me read you one or two:

> I stood in Venice, on the Bridge of Sighs;
>   A palace and a prison on each hand:
> I saw from out the wave her structures rise
>   As from the stroke of the enchanter's wand;
>   A thousand years their cloudy wings expand

Around me, and a dying glory smiles
  O'er the far times, when many a subject land
Bowed to the winged lion's marble piles
  Where Venice sat in state, throned on her hundred isles.

"But part of that I don't understand," exclaimed Willie. "What was the Bridge of Sighs, and what was the winged lion?"

THE MOLO, VENICE.

"Oh, I know all about the Bridge of Sighs," said Burt; "it is the bridge connecting the palace with the prison, and prisoners were taken across this bridge after they had been sentenced; but where is the winged lion?"

"Well, in this view you see the lion on the top of the pillar. It was the standard of Venice, and was painted on their flags. St. Mark was the patron saint. Public executions in ancient Venice were conducted between these pillars.

"Didn't the Doges used to go through some ceremony they called wedding the Adriatic?" asked Nettie.

"Yes, I thought I had a view to illustrate it, but I find I haven't. Every year the Doge was rowed out in a state boat called the Bucentaur to the Adriatic, and threw a ring into the sea. You see Venice derived her wealth from commerce. Byron speaks of this when he says:

FLORENCE.

The spouseless Adriatic mourns her lord,
And, annual marriage now no more renewed,
The Bucentaur lies rotting, unrestored—
Neglected garments of her widowhood!

As it was getting quite late, Uncle George asked Burt to point out on the map the location of Florence. You have all heard of Florence. This is the great art center of Italy. It is not only a beautiful city, but has most interesting associations. Here again we find a river—the Arno—dividing the city into two unequal parts, and here is a view looking up the river."

"What a queer looking bridge that is," said Nettie, pointing to the bridge in the immediate foreground.

"That is the Ponte Vecchio, sometimes called the Jewelers' Bridge, because there are jewelers' shops all along it. There is a singular covered passage way along the top; it joins two famous palaces, one on the north and one on the south side of the river. The Uffizi Palace on the south has one of the most famous collection of pictures and other art treasures in the world; it is impossible to describe it. The palace on the north is the Vecchi Palace; in earlier times it was the City Hall. It was built very strong, for there were troublous times in Florence. Here is a view of the court-yard. Now it is somewhat singular what a number of noted men have lived in Florence. There was Michael Angelo, who was probably the greatest artist that ever lived; there was Dante, the great poet of Italy; there was the navigator, Amerigo Vespucci."

"Oh, I know about him! This continent was named after him, wasn't it, uncle?" exclaimed Henry. "But I didn't know he lived in Florence."

"His home is still shown," continued Uncle George, "and there is a little tablet fixed on the side, stating that he lived there once. Another noted Florentine was Galileo Galilei, the great astronomer. I presume you have all heard of a noted scene in his life."

"What was it, please, uncle?" asked Ida.

"Well, you know in an early age it was supposed that the earth was fixed immovable in space, and that the sun and the stars revolved around it. Galileo knew better than this, and taught that the earth revolved around the sun. Such was the unfortunate ignorance of the times that the authorities compelled him to recant this theory. They burned his books in the public square, and, knowing that it was death if he refused, Galileo humbly declared that 'with a sincere heart and unfeigned faith, I abjure, curse, and detest the said errors. I swear for the future never to say anything, verbally or in writing, which may give rise to similar suspicions against me.' That was a pretty broad denial of the whole belief, wasn't it? But tradition has it that on rising from his knees he whispered, 'But it does move, though, for all that.'"

"Do you think they would really have put him to death if he hadn't recanted?" asked Ida. "What difference did it make, anyhow, as long as he really believed it?" she added.

TOMB OF LORENZO.

"They undoubtedly would have put him to death if he had not recanted. The world has been growing wiser the last few centuries, and we begin to see that no mere matter of belief or of scientific theory is right or wrong in itself. But they didn't think that way once. But we must pass on. Still another great man of Florence was Savonarola. He was an extremely eloquent preacher, and one of the fearless spirits that did not hesitate to speak

DEATH OF SAVONAROLA.

for truth and right. Yet he had enemies, and was put to death in the public square of Florence. He was one of the reformers before the Reformation. Thus you see that Florence can claim the citizenship of many eminent men in former times. When you read history you will learn that the Medici family of Florence exercised a great influence during the fourteenth and fifteenth centuries. Their home also was in Florence. You see I have the picture of the tomb of Lorenzo di Medicis, generally known as Lorenzo the

Magnificent. The Medici family was very rich and very powerful. Fortunately they generally used their influence to advance the revival of learning, then just beginning to take place."

"What are the two figures supposed to represent?" queried Burt, pointing to the two recumbent figures in the picture.

"They represent Evening and Dawn. In the same church there is a tomb of another member of this family, and the two similar figures there are Day and Night. This Lorenzo sent learned men into all countries to collect books and antiquities; he set up printing presses, and he adorned Florence

STREET IN POMPEII.

with buildings and gardens; but then he was a despotic ruler of Florence, for all that."

"Uncle," said Willie, "before you close for to-night, you ought to tell us something about Pompeii and its destruction."

"Oh, I heard about that place; but what destroyed it—how did it all happen?" broke in Henry.

"Pompeii and Herculaneum, Henry, were two sea-coast cities of ancient Italy, situated near the foot of Mt. Vesuvius. This is, as you know, a volcano; but it had long been quiet, and was supposed to be extinct. But in the year 79 of our era the volcano suddenly became active, and these cities were overwhelmed in the eruption. Pompeii was buried under the ashes and general debris of the outbreak. It was gradually forgotten, but in the middle of the last century it was rediscovered in digging a well. Since that time systematic attempts have been made to excavate the city. I have here a view in a street of Pompeii which has been cleared out. It will be a good many years yet before the entire city is recovered. But, as it is, most valuable results have been obtained."

At this point Uncle George again glanced at his watch and decided that it was time for the club to adjourn. So the announcement was made that the next trip was to be to Greece, and, if time allowed, to Constantinople.

"I am sorry," added Uncle George, "that we cannot devote more time to a country. But you see we have a good ways to go yet in our journey, and I am not sure that I can be with you many months longer, and I presume you will be tired of the journey by the time I am ready to go."

"Say, uncle!" exclaimed Burt, when he suddenly stopped. The fact was, he had formed a sudden determination to go with his uncle if it could be brought about. Perhaps the fact that he was so quiet and sober made the whole club quiet on the way home.

16

CHAPTER VII.

HELLAS AND THE LEVANT.

WAS kite-flying time when the sixth meeting of the club was held. No one can just tell why it is that small boys are seized with a desire to fly kites when spring comes on; but certain it is that when the March winds begin to blow, and the early flowers think it about time to make their spring opening, the boys get their kites in order. This had been the principal business with Henry for some days; and, in fact, that mysterious disease, spring fever, had taken more or less of a hold on the others as well. And so they hadn't thought very much about Greece or the East. They were, however, all ready to go to grandpa's. Though it was most too late for maple sugar, still some syrup had been saved, and they were going to have a final sugaring-off. So they assembled in the afternoon and had a good time down in the kitchen. Aunt Mary got up just the nicest little supper; but then she was famous for that sort of work. Grandpa told stories about his boyhood days; but we are not sure that, looking back through the mist of many years, his recollection was a little distorted; for in old age memory throws around childhood days a deceitful charm. Mrs. Adams, the mother of Burt and Willie, was there too. Now she did not often leave her home, and you would probably not guess what had brought her there with such a thoughtful look on her face. And what could she be talking about to Uncle George up in the library? We will tell you the secret, but be careful and don't repeat it. The fact is, Burt, who had been unusually quiet and thoughtful for several days, had finally told his mother that Uncle George was talking about going away, and he wanted to know if he couldn't go with him. We all know how such a proposition would be apt to strike his mother. At first she did not think it could be done, then she would consider it, and, finally, she would see Uncle George in reference to it. So that was her principal business at this time. When she and Uncle George got through their talk, there was a serious but satisfied look on their faces. Burt could not quite make up his mind from their looks what they had decided on. But the evening drew on, and Uncle George and the club took possession of the library. Various books and the atlas were already on the long table, and the evening's trip soon began.

"Now," commenced Uncle George, "I want you to notice the map that Burt has before him. It looks only a little ways from Italy to Greece, but in this case appearances are deceptive in more than one sense. Italy belongs to western Europe; her past history and her present trade are with Europe. But Greece looks toward the east, and her·past history and present trade belong to the East. So when we get through with Italy we start from Naples on the western shore, and go clear around Italy and around Greece to its eastern side before we stop. But this voyage is one of the pleasantest imaginable. In the early morning the shores of Greece first come in sight. All travelers have a good deal to say about the beautiful color and light in Greece. Sometimes, at rare intervals, on a hot summer's day you can see a bluish haze about a distant landscape, blending the foliage together, toning down the rocks and the hills. In Greece, and the islands off her shores, this haze effect may be seen to perfection. Sometimes all sorts of colors seem to be blended while the air is perfectly clear and the sky the deepest kind of blue. The view from the sea shows us a land broken and rugged. The mainland at Greece is deeply indented at several places by gulfs and almost land-locked bays, and is crossed and re-crossed by mountain ranges. You notice from the map that the western part of Greece is a peninsula—the Peloponnesus. This was the home of the Spartans; or perhaps I had better say the Spartans were the principal Greek people in the peninsula. Well, our ship keeps on around the peninsula and finally passes Cape Malea. Now we enter the old Greek world. Their sailors used to say, 'When you pass Cape Malea, forget your home.' I suppose I might tell you a good deal about the ancient Greeks, but it might not interest you."

"Is Greece an older country than Rome that we talked about the other night?" inquired Nettie.

"Oh, yes. Long before there was any civilization in Italy there were culture and refinement in Greece. In fact, quite a large part of the population that made the Romans came from Greece. Southern Italy at one time was known as Greater Greece. But now let us resume our course. Passing up the Gulf of Egina, we ought not to forget that all around us is most interesting historical ground. Every promontory, every island, every bay has its history. And thus to the beauty of nature is added the charm of historical and poetical association. Finally we come to anchor in the harbor of Athens called the Piræus, and I have here a view of this famous old harbor."

"And is that the city of Athens right on the shore, uncle?" spoke up Willie.

"No; that is the modern town of Piræus. This has all been built up

HARBOR OF THE PIRÆUS.

within the last fifty years. Greece used to belong to Turkey, and was terribly backward, but the country has developed quite rapidly. Athens is some five miles away. Way back in history this harbor was connected with Athens by great long walls; parts of them still remain. Their foundations, twelve feet thick, are used as the bed of the carriage road and railroad. When Athens was in her glory under Pericles, this harbor was a very strong one, and its mouth was defended by chains. By the way, I have somewhere a picture of it. Yes; here it is." And as he spoke Uncle George opened another book.

"And there are some more of those funny boats," said Henry, pointing them out. "They look as if they had duck heads on," he added.

"So they do," said Uncle George, laughing at the odd simile. "Well, we must hurry on. Though there is a railroad running up to the city, most travelers prefer to take a carriage and drive up. There is, however, nothing to remind us that we are but a few miles from one of the most interesting

ATHENS UNDER PERICLES.

cities in the world. About half way to the city there is a wayside inn, and every coachman feels it to be his bounden duty to stop here and rest a while. No matter how much of a hurry you may be in, you can not persuade them to break this custom. However, we soon arrive at Athens. Modern Athens is a finely constructed city of nearly 100,000 people, having all the modern conveniences. But, of course, the great charm of the city is its historical significance. Just think; here we are in the oldest city in Europe. Long before Rome was settled Athens was a city. For centuries it was the intellectual center of Europe. All our classical scholars point to Athens as the home of philos-

ophers, poets, and artists at a time when the rest of Europe was in a condition of semi-barbarism. So we will first of all learn a little about these old
Greeks, and see what ruins they have left
behind that will be of interest to us."

"Ain't there anything but old ruins to
see?" inquired Henry in a tone which plainly
said he didn't care much for them.

"Well, that is about all of interest,
Henry," replied Uncle George, "but I guess
we can enjoy ourselves for all that, and I am
sure all who have read history will take a
great deal of interest in them."

In fact, the rest of the club had already
expressed their opinion, so Uncle George
proceeded.

" In Greece, as in Italy, there is a legendary period."

" But, uncle," broke in Nettie, " I meant
to have asked you before, what do you mean
by a legendary period?"

" Why, a legend is any remarkable story
handed down from the past, which there is
no very good ground for believing to be true
—simply a marvelous story. Well, early
Greek history is full of such marvelous
stories, about which no one is expected to
concern himself now. This picture I have
here is about a famous expedition—the
Argonautic Expedition. Now any of you
who want to read queer stories of the mythical period in Greece, must hunt up an account of this expedition in search of the
Golden Fleece."

ARGONAUTIC EXPEDITION.

" Why don't you tell it to us, uncle?"
exclaimed Henry, always ready to hear a story.

"Oh, that would take too long, but I have shown you a picture of the ship Argo, and in the ship are supposed to be standing some of the mythical heroes—such as Hercules, Theseus, Castor, and Pollux—just starting away on their dangerous trip. But probably the greatest collection of old stories is about the siege and destruction of Troy."

"Where was that Troy, uncle? I never could find it on any map of Greece," said Burt.

"You will not find it on any map of Greece, Burt; you might find it on some of the ancient history maps of Asia Minor, for it was near the Helles-pont in Asia. Some of you older children have heard more or less of Homer, the famous poet of ancient Greece. We owe to him, or at any rate for the collection of poems under his

TROJAN WAR HEROES.

name, our first knowledge of ancient Troy. He told us about the famous Trojan War, and I see I have a picture of some of the heroes of that war as well as a picture from an old painting of Homer himself."

ΟΜΗΡΟΣ

"What is the name under that picture?" asked Nettie, slowly spelling it out.

"That picture of Homer is from an old painting or bit of sculpture, I forget which, and the Greek name for Homer is copied also."

"What was it all about, anyway?" spoke up Henry, who didn't seem to be much interested.

"Oh, well; it is extremely difficult to say how much, if any, historical truth there is in the stories of this war. All this happened way before the dawn of history. But you must all read about them some time. There are any number of charming stories connected with them. By the way, I have a picture, ' The Return from Troy.' "

" They look as if they were glad to get back," said Ida.

Uncle George smiled as he continued : " Well, now, I don't want to

RETURN FROM TROY.

keep you very long on this part. But here we have a collection of pictures representing various gods of Greek mythology. You see we have Jupiter and Juno, Neptune and Pluto, and in the center the assembly of all the gods on Mount Olympus."

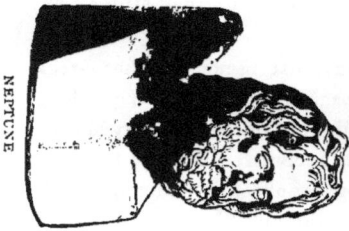

NEPTUNE

JUNO.

ASSEMBLY OF THE GODS ON MT. OLYMPUS.

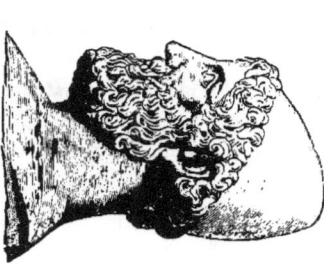

PLUTO.

JUPITER.

"How funny, ain't it, uncle, that they believed in all that stuff?" exclaimed Burt.

"Well, my boy," replied Mr. Adams, "you must remember that Greek mythology, like the stories we have just been speaking about, properly belong to the childhood period of her history. Religions always change very slowly. Probably as long back as when Greece became a civilized country the educated classes did not believe in their mythology; only the common people held to the old ideas. But the educated people did not like to disturb the

TYPES OF GREEK WOMEN.

faith of the masses; and, besides, they were influenced by the superstition of their childhood. But we must not discuss this now."

"Uncle," said Henry, who had been looking at the picture, "what are they doing in the center picture?"

"The Greeks believed that Mt. Olympus was the home of the gods. This is a council of all the gods and goddesses."

"Now, the Greeks themselves were a singular sort of people. Much has been said about the beauty of the people. I have a picture of Greek women,

GREEK FESTIVAL SCENE.

and so you can judge for yourself. But nowadays you will not see such types except in rare localities where the race has kept comparatively pure. But at the present day, as in ancient times, the people are inquisitive, nervous, vain, egotistical, and intellectual all at once. That makes rather of a singular mixture; but they always have been singular people."

"It seems as if all the people you tell us about, uncle, think they are a little smarter than the rest of the folks," said Willie.

"That is a pretty general complaint," said Mr. Adams. "All people, even we in America, are apt to think they are better than any other people.

ENTRANCE TO A GREEK GARDEN.

Extensive reading or traveling is a sure cure for this complaint. But now I have a picture supposed to represent a garden of a rich Greek in ancient times. But only a few, of course, could enjoy these luxuries. You see the slaves are in attendance, and they have music and all that."

"And they had slaves like the old Romans, did they?" added Henry.

"Yes; slavery is an old institution. The Greeks believed in enjoying themselves. I have a festival scene, but women were not present at these places. They had—especially the people of Athens—very strict ideas about keeping the women closely shut up at home; and in this respect, judging by the conduct of the present people of Athens, they are imitated by the modern Greeks. But the case was different in Sparta. Have any of you ever read about the Spartans?"

All of the older children had some vague ideas about the strange government in Sparta; but as Henry wanted to know more about it, Uncle George told them considerable about the Spartans and their strange system of government.

"Now," he resumed, " I have some views of Greek home-life in old

ENTERTAINMENT OF A GREEK LADY.

times, supposed to be in the house of a rich Greek. The lady is being entertained by musicians and dancers, and notice the toilet articles."

"How long ago was what you call 'old times' in Greece?" inquired Willie.

"Three or four centuries before Christ," replied his uncle. "You must understand," he added, "that Greece was the first country in Europe to become civilized. This was largely owing to their location—right near to Asia, you see, and thus brought in contact with the civilized people in that country. But they soon surpassed their teachers. The modern Greeks of the present day are very inquisitive. By the way, a recent traveler tells of arriving at a secluded village in Greece, and of how anxious the people were to ask him questions. The village school-master took the lead in questioning him. Here is the account, which Ida may read : "

Ida took the book which her uncle handed her, and read as follows : "If ever I regretted not being a walking encyclopedia, it was during the examination this good man put me through. All the youth of the place eagerly

ORNAMENTAL ARTICLES USED IN GREEK LIFE.

caught at my answers, and did not miss such a good opportunity of getting information. If he let me rest a moment, all his neighbors suggested new questions to him. They had to be told of France, of Paris, and our large rivers; of the railroads, of balloons, of England and China, and particularly of California. Their curiosity was not of too ignorant a nature, and their very questions showed they had a tolerable knowledge of things. They listened to my answers in murmuring silence, and passed on the answers to those that were too far off to hear me."

"Now," said Uncle George, " that brings me to the last point I want to mention about the Greek people. You see here a picture entitled ' Herodotus Reading his History.' You see the people then must have been much like the Greeks of to-day—curious to hear all that was to be said by any one who

HERODOTUS READING HISTORY.

could instruct them. It was this inquisitive nature that did much to make them renowned in arts and sciences."

"And who was this man—what did you call his name?" asked Henry, pointing to the picture.

"Herodotus; he is sometimes called the 'father of history,' one of the early Greek travelers and historians. But now let us talk about what is to

THE ACROPOLIS OF ATHENS—RECONSTRUCTION.

be seen in Athens now. I have here a view of ancient Athens, and the same picture, I might remark, would do for a bird's-eye view of modern Athens, as all the distinct outlines are there."

"And what a queer hill right in the middle of the city!" exclaimed Nettie, pointing to the Acropolis.

"That, said Uncle George, " is one of the most interesting places in the world. It is the Acropolis or citadel of Athens. It is a high rocky hill, rising some 300 feet above the level of the city; the top was leveled and the sides made precipitous by artificial means. Then the top was further protected by a wall, and public buildings were erected on it. Wonderful interest is associated with all these buildings, and when you gaze on the ruins you

ANCIENT ATHENS.

must remember that the buildings were erected more than 400 years B. C. A recent writer says: 'Not Rome with its Forum and Colosseum, nor Baalbec with its Temple of the Sun, nor Pompeii with its revised association, nor Ephesus with its wondrous theater and Temple of Diana, can be compared with the Acropolis at Athens, where even in ruins the perfection of art is enthroned.' As this is such an important place, I will show you a view of it when it was perfect."

"Uncle, won't you tell us a little more about those buildings there?" asked Burt, pointing to the picture.

"Well, we are supposed to be looking from the west. The rock was inaccessible in all other directions. Notice the path leading up to the temple-looking gateway? That is the Propylæa. The roadway leading to

17

this gateway was once lavishly decorated wtth statues and reliefs. I assure you it is very interesting to wander along this way in its present ruined state and notice the ruts in the pavement formed there more than 2,000 years ago; and as you enter the gateway, glancing back, you are afforded a most beautiful view of the distant sea flecked with islands, and the mournfully interesting ruins around."

"What is that statue of a woman there?" asked Henry.

"The Propylæa," continued Uncle George, scarcely noticing the question, "had two wings on the north and south sides respectively. Near the one on the north side was placed the celebrated statue of Athens—Promachus—

THE PARTHENON AT ATHENS.

made by Phidias. It was sixty-four feet in height, in full armor, leaning on a lance. The extremity of the lance was gilded, and formed a land-mark for sailors, as it could be seen a long way from the shore."

"Wasn't the Parthenon on the Acropolis?" queried Burt.

"Yes; that is the principal building you see in the picture. It is said that it was the finest edifice on the finest site in the world, hallowed by the noblest recollections. It was surrounded by porticoes and colonnades. This small cut will give you an idea of the building. Of course, it is in ruins now. Many of the carvings you see are now in the British Museum. When Greece was a part of Turkey, Lord Elgin, then embassador to Turkey from England, received permission from Turkey to remove them. The Greeks never forgave England for taking them, but it must be said they seem to care very little for the many interesting ruins in their midst."

"I suppose some of the columns are still standing," observed Nettie.

"Yes; thirty-six are, or at least were standing a few years ago. That building has had a curious history. For the first 1,000 years of its existence it was a temple to the virgin goddess Athene; then the Catholic Church made of it a cathedral of the Virgin Mary; then the Turks turned it into a mosque, and at present it is simply one of the grandest ruins in the world."

"Whom did you say it was dedicated to at first?" inquired Willie.

"To the titulary goddess of Athens —Athene. And, by the way, I have here a small picture of a celebrated statue of this goddess, which stood within the central hall of the Parthenon. This was one of the most celebrated statues of antiquity. It was forty-seven feet high; made of gold and ivory."

"After Phidias," said Henry, reading the title to the picture, "what does that mean?" he inquired.

"Phidias was the name of the artist who made the statue," replied Uncle George. "He was one of the most cele-brated artists that Greece produced. We will have occasion to glance at one more work of this artist before we get through with Greece."

PALLAS ATHENE, AFTER PHIDIAS.

"There is one more building that you have not told us about; what about that, uncle?" asked Burt.

"That is the Erechtheium; from the very earliest times a temple stood on that spot. But we must pass on. All over the top of the Acropolis

there are fragments of columns, pedestals, and old foundations, forming parts
of ancient buildings or celebrated statues which we can not now describe.
But you can now see why the Acropolis takes up such an important place in
our description of Athens. Now," resumed Uncle George, turning the pages
of the book he held in his hand, "we must hurry on. I see that our next
view is that of a famous Greek temple at Ægina."

"What kind of a temple is that, uncle?" inquired Burt, pointing to the
title.

"Pan-Hellenic means all of Greece; or, in other words, this was the

TEMPLE OF THE PAN-HELLENIC ZEUS AT ÆGINA.

temple to the national god of Greece. Ægina, I might remark, was an island
off the coast of Greece. You notice the pillars in front? They are Doric
pillars. The architecture of ancient Greece is quite an interesting study,
but we must not stop to consider it now. You have probably heard of the
names of the three principal orders of pillars—the Corinthian, Ionic, and
Doric."

"Corinthian," slowly pronounced Willie, "wasn't there a city of Corinth
in Greece?"

"Yes, indeed; Corinth was quite a rich and influential city on the little isthmus joining the Peloponnesus to the mainland. In the first century this was quite a celebrated place. You know in the New Testament Paul wrote two letters to the church in Corinth, but nowadays there are only a few pillars left to show that a city once stood there."

"And wasn't Paul in Athens once?" asked Nettie.

"Why, yes; he made his famous address from Mars' Hill. I was just going to speak about that place. To the west and a little to the north of the

COURT OF THE AREOPAGUS.

Acropolis is another interesting hill, sometimes, or generally in older histories, called the Areopagus, but it is also known as Mars' Hill. It got its first name from the fact that a famous court met there—the Areopagus— and I have a small cut here which shows the court in session."

"What kind of a court was it?" inquired Willie.

"Well, we know very little of these far-away times. It was a judicial body, and was especially concerned with criminal proceedings. It held its sessions in the open air, and the greatest solemnity was observed."

"Now here, perhaps, is a good place to speak of some of the great men of Athens. About a mile from the Acropolis is one of the most interesting spots in Athens.   It is an olive grove, or rather the remains of one, where Socrates and Plato taught their philosophy some four centuries before Christ. I have here a picture of Socrates and of his death.   I am sure there is no one who can read an account of the life of Socrates without admiring him. He accomplished a great work for Greek thought."

DEATH OF SOCRATES.

"Didn't I read somewhere that he had to drink a cup of poison?" inquired Ida.

"Yes, he was charged with immorality—with spreading a disbelief in the gods of Greece. But a short distance to the southwest of the Acropolis is a place called the prison of Socrates—a sort of cell hewn out in the solid rock; but there is no good reason for believing this was the place where he drank the cup of poison. In the picture you notice he is represented as about to take the cup. He could easily have fled from the country, but that he refused

290   CROESUS ON THE FUNERAL PYRE.

to do. He is supposed to have been consoling his friends, arguing that there must be a life beyond the grave, and is now ready to die."

"What about this next picture?" exclaimed Henry, who was evidently willing to hurry things along.

"Well, they tell a good story about that picture. Solon was the wise man of ancient Greece, who is supposed to have arranged their laws. He then went traveling and visited Crœsus, who was enormously wealthy. King

SOLON AND CRŒSUS.

Crœsus showed Solon his royal treasures, and incidentally remarked that he ought to be a very happy man. But the wise Athenian ventured to suggest that he could not judge of the happiness of a life until it was ended, as calamities might overtake us. He then went away. Subsequently Crœsus was conquered by his enemy and condemned to death. The views I have represent him showing his treasures to Solon, and also on the funeral pyre. One version of the story is, however, that he was saved from death. I see," remarked Uncle George, turning the page of his book, "that I have here a picture of another noted Greek, though celebrated in quite another direction.

You have heard of Alexander the Great.   Here is a picture of him as a youth with his celebrated tutor, Aristotle."

"I didn't know that Aristotle had anything to do with Alexander," said Burt.

" He was his tutor, and I suppose that it was owing to this circumstance that Aristotle owed some of his discoveries.   You see, when Alexander set out to conquer the world, he remembered his old teacher, and accordingly

ALEXANDER AND ARISTOTLE.

sent great collections of plants and animals to him to study.   The career of Alexander was a most singular one.   It illustrates one very important point. The conqueror of the world could not control his own spirit.   You know the Bible says, 'He that ruleth his own spirit is greater than he that taketh a city.'   It was surely so in his case.   Now we could talk about a great many other noted men of ancient Greece, but our time is getting short.   However, we can not leave Greece without speaking of the Olympic Games."

"Oh, yes; I thought there was something about the games I wanted to ask you about," said Burt.

"The Olympic games were great public festivals. The Greeks were very fond of such festival gatherings, and especially were they fond of the Olympic games cele-brated every four years at Olympia. The occa-sion was made a time of general peace. Heralds proclaimed throughout Greece the 'Truce of God' and all warfare ceased. As the time approached, a great stream of visitors from all parts of Greece gathered at Ellis; that was the town near where they were cele-brated. All the Greek states sent deputies clad in their robes of office. The athletes who were to take part arrived some time be-fore the opening of the festival, and underwent a course of training in the grove of Altis or sacred grove. By the way, I have a view of it here. Looks like a pleasant place, don't it?"

GROVE OF ALTIS.

"What did they do at the games, themselves?" inquired Henry.

"Oh, all sorts of athletic exercises—running, leaping, jumping, boxing, wrestling, etc. The chariot races were especially exciting. You see I have a view here supposed to represent a chariot race."

As he said this, uncle turned the page of the album and showed them a picture of the chariot race in the Olympic games. Henry asked if the chariots they had were like those in Rome. Uncle George said they were,

OLYMPIC GAMES.

and explained that the Greeks, like the Romans, were extravagantly fond of races; and, in fact, of all kinds of athletic exercises, and it was considered a great honor to win in these contests.

"What did the one get who beat?" inquired Henry.

"Nothing but a wreath of leaves from the sacred olive tree. But then other results followed. Heralds proclaimed his name and honors. If he was an Athenian, he received a small sum of money and free rations for life at the public expense. If he was a Spartan, he had the post of honor in battle. I guess we wouldn't think that a very desirable reward, but the old Spartans thought differently; with them, war was everything. You must understand that these games were of a religious character. You notice the Temple of Olympian Zeus in the picture?"

"And wasn't there a celebrated statue of some god there?" asked Burt. "It seems to me I have read about one there."

"Yes, you are right. In the temple was the celebrated statue of the Olympian Zeus. Here is a picture of it, made, you see, by that same Phidias we talked about. By the way, this was reckoned one of the seven wonders of the ancient world. The finished work was over forty feet high, and represented the god seated on his throne. On his head was a wreath of

OLYMPIAN ZEUS, AFTER PHIDIAS.

olive. The drapery was of gold, richly worked with flowers and figures in enamel. The throne was of ebony and ivory, inlaid with precious stones. Every one in Greece was expected to see that statue once, at least, in his life-time."

"Uncle," inquired Nettie, "was the Delphic Oracle at that place?"

"What was that?" added Henry.

"No; the Delphic Oracle was at Delphi. In those days of ignorance, when superstition was so very common, the gods in which they believed were supposed to have their special holy places and priests, to whom they made their wishes and intentions known in some way. Well, the special shrine of Apollo was at Delphi. There was a cleft in the rocks, and some kind of gas came up from the interior of the earth. The priestess was placed right over the cleft on a sort of tripod and was excited by the fumes, and when in that state gave out the 'oracles' that are the answers supposed to be given by the god to various questions asked him. I have a picture here to illustrate that subject."

THE PRIESTESS OF APOLLO AT DELPHI.

"Uncle, you said a while ago that the educated people probably believed in something different, what was it?" asked Burt.

"Well, I will just barely mention it, especially as I have a picture or two to illustrate it. The educated people of the world in the time of Christ held to a belief different from the ordinary masses of people. But, for various reasons, they did not think it best to teach this publicly. So they had what they called mysteries. The knowledge taught was revealed only to the initiates. The town of Eleusis, near Athens, was especially celebrated as the center of the Eleusinian mysteries. Here is a view of one of the processions held at that time. The Greeks were greatly devoted to these mysteries. It required a year to take the various degrees. Only the full-fledged members took part in the procession represented in this picture. If any one

ELEUSINIAN FEAST.

neglected initiation into them, they were held in about the same light that we hold an infidel at the present day. That was one of the complaints against Socrates. When you get older, you must read up about these

Elusinian mysteries.   And I have also one of the symbolical pictures of an old mythological event that they worked over and made the means of teaching their new truths. Now, I must leave this subject, for, though one of the greatest interest to the student, I think we can find something more interesting to talk about. Perhaps we have spent all the time necessary on Greeee. So we will leave that land and hurry on further east. We must look at a few views of Constantinople yet. Henry, can't you tell me how we go from Greece to Constantinople?"

"Why, we take a ship at Athens, and, after passing Greece, go off northeast across the Ægean Sea, and then we come to the Dardanelles and the Sea of Marmora, and then the Bosphorus, and there we are."

"I believe that is about the right way, Henry; though we had better make sure by glancing at the map that Burt has. But we will suppose that we have arrived in front of Constantinople. As you approach the city the scenery is certainly grand. I have a picture here which gives us a faint idea of it. On the one side of that narrow stream of water is Europe; on the other, Asia. The hills are crowded with buildings. You must understand that what we call Constantinople is really three cities. Stamboul and Galata on the European side; between them, in the little inlet of the Golden Horn on the Asiatic shore, we have Scutari. With this picture before us,

RAPE OF PERSEPHONE.

VIEW OF CONSTANTINOPLE.

18

let Ida read this description by the Italian traveler, Amicis," said Uncle George, handing her the description.

It had been quite a while since Ida had read any for the club, but she read quite nicely the following account: "The Golden Horn is directly before us like a river; on either shore two chains of heights on which rise and lengthen out two parallel chains of cities, embracing eight miles of hills, valleys, bays, and promontories; a hundred amphitheaters of monuments and gardens, houses, mosques, bazaars of an infinite variety of colors; in the midst thousands of minarets with shining pinnacles rising into the sky like columns of ivory; groves of cypress trees descending in long lines from the heights to the sea. To the right, Galata, faced by a forest of masts and sails and flags. Above Galata, Pera; the vast outlines of her European palaces drawn upon the sky; in front a bridge connecting the two shores, and traversed by two throngs of many colored people. To the left, Stamboul stretched upon her broad hills, upon each of which rises a gigantic mosque with leaden dome and golden pinnacles; behind you the shores of Asia close the panorama with the pompous splendors of Scutari."

"That is very good," said Uncle George, when she ceased reading. "However, of all these places, distance lends enchantment to the view; when you land and walk around, you do not find as much to admire. For the streets are narrow and dirty; there is a general appearance of indolence. The Turks believe in letting events take their course, and in many respects are away behind the present times. But the natural scenery is lovely; the shores are bluffy, and so the appearance at a distance is very striking. But, changing the subject, can any of you tell me whom Constantinople was named after?"

It was Burt who answered the query by naming Constantine the Great. And then Uncle George told them about its being for a long while the capital of the eastern division of the Roman Empire, and of its final taking by the Turks, in whose hands it has since remained.

"You notice in the background," resumed Uncle George, "a point of land with a number of steeples, or minarets as the Turks call them; that is known as Seraglio Point, and is the very heart of Constantinople. Until very recently the Sultan had his residence there. It was a most splendid building, but his favorite palace is now outside of the city proper on the shores of the Bosphorus."

"If he had such a nice place, what made him want to leave it?" asked Henry.

"Well, he wanted a change, and so he had a magnificent palace built along the shore of the Bosphorus. Here is a view of it. You see it is right on the banks of the Bosphorus. It fronts along the shore for nearly half a mile. There are more than twenty splendid buildings constituting this

DOLMA BAGHTCHE.

palace. It may give you an idea of its vastness to learn that it requires the services of 5,500 servants to keep it in order. There are 400 boatmen, 400 musicians, and others in proportion. In the royal stables there are some 600 horses, 200 carriages, etc. All this, of course, requires an immense outlay of money. So it is no wonder that Turkey is practically bankrupt all the time. It is a wonderfully corrupt and extravagant government, and it don't seem as though it could maintain itself much longer in Europe."

ROOM IN THE SERAGLIO.

"Who will get Constantinople then?" asked Willie.

"That question can hardly be answered now. Russia has been longing for it for two centuries; and if it was not for the rest of Europe, she would undoubtedly have taken it before this time."

"What stops her?" asked Henry. "Ain't she strong enough to do it?" he added, referring, of course, to Russia and the conquest of Constantinople.

"Well, none of the great powers of Europe want Russia to secure possession of Constantinople. You see that would make Russia very much stronger. So Austria, Germany, and the other powers are ready to help Turkey. By this means the Turks manage to keep possession of their territory. I notice I have a picture here of a room in the old palace at Seraglio Point. That will give us an idea of Oriental luxury. Notice the fountain playing in the room, and the immense windows looking out on the water? The trimmings are of the very richest description. The wood work is inlaid with gold, ivory, and precious stones."

"What are they sitting on?" asked Henry.

"A sort of raised mat or couch runs around the room near the windows, and, like all Turks, they are sitting cross-legged. We wouldn't fancy sitting that way very long; but a Turk will sit that way for hours at a time smoking his pipe, apparently enjoying himself to the utmost. I suppose if the walls of that palace could speak, they would tell us much interesting history. When the Turks first appeared in Europe, it seemed as if they were destined to carry everything before them. They came very near capturing Vienna once, and, had they succeeded, history would probably have been a little different during the last century. The king of Poland, however, came to the rescue, and they were driven back. The most thoughtful of the Turks now regard it as only a question of time when they will be driven out of Europe altogether. But let us return to our pictures. This palace that we were looking at a minute ago is some miles up the Bosphorus; by the way, Henry, do you know what bodies of water that strait connects?"

Uncle George did not catch Henry on that question. Henry was, as he expressed it, solid on geography, and quickly answered that it was the Sea of Marmora and the Black Sea.

"Now, I might as well call your attention to this strait. It is probably the most interesting one in the world, as far as scenery is concerned. After looking at this view of a lovely little suburb a few miles from Constantinople, Willie may read this account of the scenery."

After glancing at the picture of Buyukdere, Willie read the following extract: "Probably no spot in the world exceeds in beauty the banks of the Bosphorus. There is an endless succession of pictures, sublime and

BUYUKDERE.

beautiful, delicate and gorgeous in coloring, soft and rugged by turns. Nor is it nature alone that charms. The sweeping lines of cupolas and graceful minarets meet the eye everywhere; the waters are alive with innumerable craft; and palaces, terraces, kiosks, castles, and shady groves are reflected on the water as in a mirror. More than this, every yard of either bank is historic ground. Every era in the world's history has left its mark on the banks of this famous strait. Here the civilization of the East sought a bridge into the West. Innumerable stories might be told of mythological times and beings; of the Phalanxes of Darius; the 10,000 warriors of Xenophon; the crusading multitudes of the pious Godfrey men who passed in successive ages across this stream, which gives to history some of its most splendid stories, and which concentrates still upon its waters the interests and the fate of empires."

"Some of the parties named," resumed Uncle George, "Darius, Xenophon, and Godfrey, are probably unknown to you; but what Willie read will help you form an idea of the historic interest and beauty of this strait. But now let us get back to the city itself. In this view I show you the principal mosque of Constantinople and one of the most celebrated churches in the Orient—the mosque of St. Sophia. There are four high minarets or spires;

ST. SOPHIA AT CONSTANTINOPLE.

only two, you see, are shown in the picture. When you enter the church, it is seen to be a very grand one. The immense dome seems suspended in air. There are many pillars, enormous arches, and a real forest of columns. Some of the pillars are objects of interest. Eight of them came from the Temple of the Sun at Baalbec; others from the Temple of Diana at Ephesus; and still others from Palmyra, Thebes, Rome, Athens, and Alexandria."

"How came they to get in the church or mosque?" asked Ida.

"Justinian, who built the church of St. Sophia, was one of the last great

Emperors of Rome. He exerted all his power to build a magnificent church, one that would be an ornament to his capital. He proudly exclaimed when he had finished it, 'Solomon, I have surpassed thee;' meaning that the church which he had built was grander than the Temple of Solomon at Jerusalem. By the way, there is a walled-up door in the church, about which such an interesting story is told that Ida may read it," saying which, Uncle George handed Ida a book opened where he had placed a mark

Ida then read the following story: "At the moment when the Turks broke into the Church of St. Sophia, a Greek bishop was saying mass before the high altar. At the sight of the invaders he abandoned the altar, went into the gallery, and disappeared through this little door before the eyes of the pursuing soldiers, who instantly found themselves stopped by a stone wall. They began to pound furiously upon the wall, but only succeeded in leaving the marks of their weapons upon it. Masons were called; but, after having worked for a whole day with pick and mattock, were obliged to renounce the task. All the masons in Constantinople tried their hands at it, and all failed to open a breach in the miraculous wall. But that wall will open; it will open on the day when the profaned basilica shall be restored to Christian worship. Then the Greek bishop will issue forth, dressed in his pontifical habit with the chalice in his hand, with a radiant countenance, and, mounting the steps of the high altar, he will resume the mass at the exact point where he left off, and on that day the dawn of new centuries shall shine resplendent for Constantinople."

"But that ain't true, is it uncle?" exclaimed Henry, who had listened with a great deal of interest to the story.

"Well, I guess it won't do to believe it all," said Uncle George, smiling.

"I wish you would tell us more about the fall of Constantinople, uncle," said Burt.

"I am quite willing to do that," replied his uncle. "Constantinople was the capital of the Eastern Division of the Roman Empire. As the power of that empire dwindled it concentrated itself more and more around Constantinople, until finally that city was about all that was left of the once great Empire of Rome. The Mohammedan power in Asia Minor had for some centuries desired to gain Constantinople, but they had not been strong enough to do this until the Turks appeared on the scene, who soon became the ruling people of the Mohammedan Empire. But it was not until the middle of the sixteenth century that they were able to effect their wish in this matter. Then they made use of cannon for the first time in modern warfare. There was a terrible conflict around the walls of Constantinople, but the Turks were successful. With the fall of Constantinople the Roman Empire disappeared from the world."

It was just at this moment that the clock struck nine, which was the hour that the club generally adjourned. So Uncle George made a few remarks, and told them that the next evening would be taken up in talking about people and scenes in Asia.

"We will take an entirely new start," he said. "Instead of going east we will go off west across the Pacific Ocean, and talk a little about China, Japan, and India; that will be a change."

The children were soon on the way home, and Henry went fast asleep before he had gone very far from grandpa's. Burt was wondering whether he was going with his uncle on his next trip, and the rest were more or less thinking of the events of the evening.

SOCRATES.

CHAPTER VIII.

EASTERN ASIA.

IS hard to decide what season of the year we most enjoy; the love of change makes us welcome each as it comes. And then, besides, each has its particular charms. Fruitful summer, picturesque autumn, snowy winter, floral spring— how true it is that we welcome their coming and speed their going. While that is true, probably the children would decide that, all things considered, spring was the most enjoyable season of the year. And if we would only question Mother Nature we would discover the reason for this. Then the year itself is young, and so is sympathetic with youth. Now, when the club met for its seventh session, April, with its singing birds and opening flowers, was well under way; so it was probably a good thing that Uncle George had something new to attract them. They were going to bid good-bye to Europe and go in a new direction. Henry said that Europe was " getting old," and possibly the other children shared this feeling in a measure. But, as it was, they were quite ready to go to grandpa's when the time arrived for the meeting. The days were rapidly growing in length at that time of the year, and it was just getting dark when they arrived. There was also one new sensation to talk about. It was now an open secret that, if Uncle George went away in the summer, Burt was to go along. You can imagine what an important personage that made him. His brother Willie was at first inclined to think he ought to go. But, after talking with his mother about it, he felt quite resigned. As he said, they couldn't both go, and he was going to have a good time at home, anyway.

When they reached the library, they found an entirely new set of books on the table, and Uncle George had some funny looking objects in his hand which had a decided Chinese look to them. The lamps were lit, and the evening's trip begun by Uncle George asking Henry a few questions about the Pacific Ocean.

VIEW OF TOKIO.

312

"Now," said he, "we will have to hurry along to-night. And so we will suppose that we have crossed this big ocean, of which Henry was telling us just now, and have arrived at Japan. As you all know, Tokio is the capital of Japan, so I will first show you a view in that city."

"But, uncle, I thought the capital was Yeddo," exclaimed Nettie.

"Yeddo is the old name, it belongs to old Japan; but Tokio is the new name," replied her uncle.

"Oh, that is Yeddo that used to be in our old geographies, is it?" said Burt. "Why, I thought that Yeddo was a great big place. That don't look like much of a city. What made them change its name, uncle?"

"The change of name is only an illustration of what has been going on in Japan the last twenty years. The whole nation has been seized with a feverish desire of change, which I will talk about soon. As for the size of the place, it was greatly exaggerated in the past. Still it is much larger than it looks. Ida, you read for us this little extract about Tokio," handing her a book with a marked passage.

"No view of Tokio is striking," commenced Ida; "there is a monotony of meanness about it. The hills are not heights, and there are no salient objects to detain the eye for an instant. As a city, it lacks concentration. Masses of greenery, lined or patched with gray, and an absence of beginning or end, look suburban rather than metropolitan. Far away in the distance are other gray patches. You are told that those are still Tokio, and you ask no more. You can drive in a crooked line fifteen miles from north to south, and eleven miles from west to east, and are still in Tokio. The blue waters of the gulf are its only recognizable boundary. It is an aggregate of one hundred and twenty-five villages which grew together round the great fortress of the Mikado's chief vassal, and which, while retaining their parks, country houses, gardens, lakes, streams and fields, their rustic lanes and sylvan beauty, have agreed to call themselves Tokio."

"Ain't that a mountain off to one side?" asked Henry, pointing to the picture.

"Yes, that is the Mountain of Fujisan. Like the Acropolis of Athens, that mountain is sure to appear in the background of any picture of Tokio. But all around the city itself is a dreary flat plain, where enormous quantities of rice are raised. Rice, by the way, is the great staple of food with the Japanese. I have just spoken about the wonderful advance in all directions

that Japan has made but recently. Well, a few years ago there was a strange
sort of government. The Mikado, the imperial ruler, lived in Tokio; but
another officer, the military chief, called the Shogun, was the real ruler.
Then the aristocracy of the land consisted of several hundred Daimios,
chiefs of tribes. Here we have a view of one of the palaces in Tokio where
the Daimios used to live once on a time."

"Uncle, what made all this change?" inquired Willie.

OLD PALACE, TOKIO.

"It is most too long to answer that question in full. I need only say
that this double government has been abolished; the Mikado is the sole
ruler; the Daimios voluntarily surrendered their power. The government
invited foreigners in to teach them; schools were established; enterprising
young Japanese boys were sent to schools in America and Europe; railroads
were built; telegraph lines opened; the army was reorganized; a navy built;

and so almost at a bound Japan passed from a semi-barbaric state into full
civilization. But it remains to be seen whether this state of things will last.

JAPANESE COURT DRESS.

You can not change the manners and customs of a people in a day, and a
great many wise people think they can see signs of a re-action coming on.
Here is a view of a courtier in full dress; however, you must understand that

19

that is true only of the old times I was speaking about. They are not in style now. The upper classes affect the European style of dressing, and probably before many years the distinctively national dress will disappear except in rural districts."

"I don't see how he could walk," said Ida, looking at the picture.

"They had to shuffle along the best way they could. Of course, you

JAPANESE WEDDING.

understand that was only the court dress. If you should happen ·to be in Tokio on a festival day, you would greatly admire the holiday clothes ; but if a rain storm should come up, you would soon make another discovery—the fine clothes are nothing but paper. Veils, headgear, mantles, all begin to grow pulpy, and soon are not fit to wear. There is this much consolation about it, they only cost a few cents to begin with. Our next view," continued Uncle George, " is that of a Japanese wedding."

"What are they all sitting on the floor for?" asked Henry.

"Why, chairs, sofas, tables, stools, and similar articles to sit on are unknown luxuries in Japan. The floors are covered with nice mats, made of a uniform size. When you enter a house, you are expected to leave your boots or shoes at the door. The natives sit down very comfortably—cross-legged—but we would be apt to complain of cramp before many minutes."

"There don't seem to be much in the room, anyway," added Ida.

"No, you need not look for a great amount of furniture," replied Uncle George. "When a young couple set up housekeeping, all they need is a few mats for the floor, two sorts of thick quilts for bedding, a pan to cook rice in, a few large cups and trays, and a bath-tub. As rice is the principal article of food, they live very economically. Take them all in all, the Japanese are a very peculiar people. Ida may read for us this condensed account of Japanese customs."

Ida then read the following account: "Politeness is a national characteristic. The foreigner in Japan is surprised to hear the politest phrases and to see mutual forbearance among the commonest coolies. Indeed, the Japanese make no distinction between politeness and morals. They say that cheating, lying, and other moral misdeeds are not polite. The people are, in general, neat and clean in their houses, persons, and dress. Tea is a universal beverage, and is served on all occasions in cups holding about half a gill, which are drained many times during the day. Smoking is general among men and women. The visitor is always served with tea, sweetmeats laid on a white paper on a tray, and a little bowl with a live coal in it to light his pipe with. Chop-sticks, as in China, take the place of the knife and fork. Food is eaten out of lacquered wooden bowls and porcelain cups. A feast is accompanied by music and dancing, and the last of the many courses is rice and tea. Sake or rice beer is served throughout the feast; it is kept in tall bottles, which are first set in boiling water to heat the sake, which is always drank hot. The cups used at a feast are very small, and are passed around or thrown across to each other by the guests, and filled by pretty damsels in waiting. At a banquet, any one can introduce himself to another person by offering the cup; if he drinks and returns the cup, the introduction is made and acquaintance begins. The houses are low, and built of a frame of wood with wattling of reed or bamboo; the interstices filled with mud, and covered with white plaster."

"I only want to add to that long extract," said Uncle George, as Ida concluded, "that, in general, the people are very light-hearted and merry,

JAPANESE BALANCING FEATS.

and believe in having a thoroughly good time. They are very fond of shows of all kinds, and especially feats of balancing and jugglery. Now here I have a picture of jugglers performing some wonderful tricks in balancing."

VIEW OF TIEN TSIN.

"What in the world, uncle, is that thing they are standing on?" broke in Willie.

"That is a false nose; it is a bamboo pole fixed on the face right over the nose. Just see that fellow standing on one, playing with the balls and keeping the parasol revolving all at once! I thought," resumed Uncle George, after they had all examined the picture as much as they wished, "that we would only just pause at Japan and hurry on to other parts of Eastern Asia, so we will talk a little about China now. Just turn the page of the atlas, Burt, and you see China. It is, as you all know, a great big country in Eastern Asia. And it is also one about whose history and general

CHINESE JUNK.

customs we are still very ignorant. It has only been about thirty years since foreigners were allowed in the country. In the first place, you may examine this picture of Tientsin at the mouth of the Pei-ho River. You notice the river emptying into the Yellow Sea (speaking more especially to Burt, who pointed it out to the rest). The capital of China, Pekin, is situated on that river."

"What kind of boats are those, uncle?" inquired Nettie.

'They are what are called junks. I believe I have a picture of one under full sail. Yes, here it is. They are rather clumsy things and the sails are made of matting, so they cannot handle them very well. Now, suppose we had landed at Tientsin, we would find any number of funny things to talk about. Their customs are exactly the reverse of ours in many ways. I have here a little extract from a book; the author is supposed to note some of his first impressions, and, as Ida reads it, you notice in how many little ways their customs differ from ours. The writer is supposed to be just getting into the port of Macao :

"On inquiring of the boatman in which direction Macao lay, I was answered 'in the *west-north*,' the wind being, as I was informed, in the *east-south*. We do not say so in Europe, thought I. But imagine my surprise, when, in explaining the utility of the compass, the boatman added that 'the needle pointed to the *south*.' Desirous to change the subject, I remarked that I concluded he was about to proceed to some high festival or merry-making, as his dress was completely *white*. He told me, with a look of much dejection, that his only brother had died the week before, and that he was in the deepest *mourning* for him. On my landing, the first object that attracted my attention was a military mandarin, who wore an embroidered

A MANDARIN.

petticoat with a string of *beads* around his neck, and who, besides, carried a fan; and it was with some dismay that I observed him mount on the *right* side of his horse."

At this point Uncle George interrupted the reading to show them the picture of a Chinese mandarin, after which Ida continued:

"At that moment my attention was drawn to several *old* Chinese, some of whom had gray beards, and nearly all of them huge goggling spectacles. A few of them were chirruping and chuckling to singing birds which they

STREET IN CHINA

carried in bamboo cages or perched on a stick; others were catching flies to feed the birds; the remainder of the party seemed to be delightedly employed in flying paper kites, while a group of *boys* were gravely looking on and regarding these innocent occupations of their seniors with the most serious and gratified attention."

There was a general laugh at this point. Henry didn't believe that he would look quietly on while his papa played with a kite. Ida then read the few remaining lines: "The next morning found me provided with a Chinese master, who happily understood English. He commenced by saying, 'When you receive a distinguished guest, do not fail to place him on the *left* hand, for that is the seat of honor; and be cautious not to *uncover* the head, as it would be an unbecoming act of *familiarity*.' Hardly prepared for this blow to my established notions, I requested he would discourse of their philosophy. He opened the volume and read with becoming gravity, 'The most learned men are decidedly of the opinion that the seat of the human understanding is the *stomach*.'"

"That account," added Uncle George, as Ida ceased reading, "is, of course, more or less a fancy one. But you will hear funny expressions. They are inquisitive, and are apt to ask such questions as 'Are your venerable parents living?' or, 'What is your sublime belief?' or, 'What is your honorable age?' or, 'What is your distinguished name?' If you happen to notice a Chinaman with a little boy of whom he is evidently very proud, you will hear him calling it 'little stupid,' or 'vagabond,' or some such a name as that. But in this case their object is to fool the evil spirit. They believe if they can only make him think they care nothing for the child he will not molest it. But we must hurry on. Here is a street scene in a Chinese city."

"Why, how narrow it is!" said Nettie, referring to the street.

"Indeed, it seems so to us. Willie, here are a few extracts about street scenes in China; read them for us, please."

"The traveler," read Willie, "as he passes along the street, finds that even the widest and busiest are narrower than our ordinary lanes. Stretch out your arms and reflect that in so doing, in an ordinary Chinese town, you would generally be able to touch the counters of the shops on both sides of the way. They have no sidewalks, and are paved with irregular stone slabs. A pretty vista of bright coloring meets our eyes, formed by the sign boards, which hang down perpendicularly from the eaves." (Here Burt silently pointed to them in the picture.) "Many of them are eight or ten feet long, and are nicely varnished and inscribed with some high-flown epithet which has been chosen by the owner instead of his name. We meet with a furrier's shop bearing the title, 'Virtuous and Abundant;' or a cloth store called 'Celestial Advantage.' An undertaker had chosen the title of 'United and Prosperous,' and a coal merchant called his premises by the high-sounding

OFFICIAL IN HIS PALANQUIN.

name of 'Heavenly Adornment.' And here are the names of some of the streets themselves—'Lane of Filial Piety,' 'Court of Eternal Harmony,' 'Street of Heavenly Treasures.'"

"The street looks as if it had a roof over it," observed Burt.

"That is a sort of frame work of bamboo, and in summer time mats are hung thereon to protect from the sun. Now notice this picture of an official chair, and let Willie continue his reading."

"No carts or carriages are seen in Chinese streets, but sedan chairs are in constant use; varying in size and appearance from the official's roomy and elaborately decorated conveyance to the fragile bamboo erections waiting for hire on the corners of the street. The official sits at ease in his richly decorated sedan chair. He wears handsome robes of satin, and an expression of impassive superiority rests upon his solemn countenance. At the head of

TSIEN MEN GATE.

the procession are small boys with large painted boards, on which are some such expressions as 'Stand aside;' or, 'Let there be respectful silence.'"

"Ain't there any big nice houses and wide streets in Pekin?" asked Ida.

"Certainly; I was just going to speak about them. Pekin is really a double city. The southern and larger part is the Chinese city proper. To the north of it is the Tartar City. Here is a gate leading from one to the other. You must understand that the ruling dynasty in China is Tartar. They conquered China some 200 years ago; and, by the way, the queue or pig-tail of which the Chinese are now so proud, is said to have been in the first place a sign of conquest. The Chinese are said to have been compelled to wear it by their Tartar conquerors. But, be that as it may, going through that gate we would find ourselves in the Tartar City with much wider streets. But within the Tartar City there is another subdivision set off by walls, in which are the palaces of the great chiefs, parks and pleasure grounds; and,

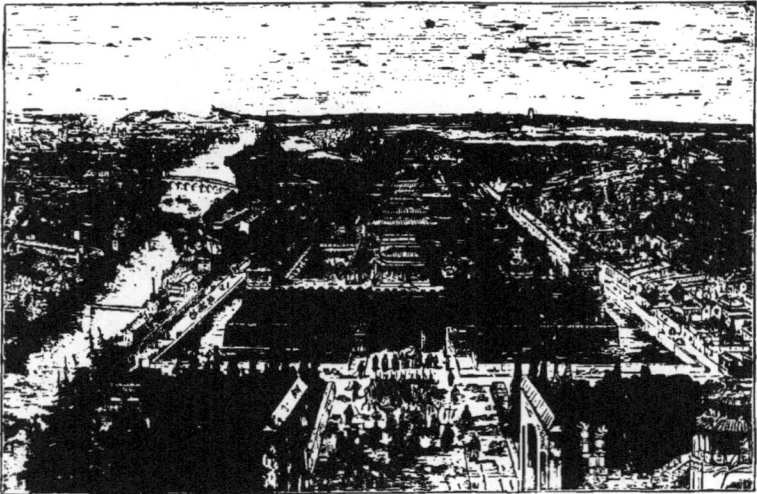

THE IMPERIAL CITY.

finally, within that still a third subdivision, shown in this cut. This is called the 'Red' or 'Prohibited City,' and is exclusively set apart for the Emperor and his court."

"Don't the boys play any games?" asked Henry, keeping in mind what Ida read about the boys looking on while the old men flew kites.

"Oh, yes, of course;" said Uncle George, "that extract was overdrawn. Boys will be boys even in China; though the whole aim of education is to make them sober and sedate, they fly kites as well as the older people, play with balls, play blind man's buff, and have great sport in turning the dragon."

"What is that?" inquired Henry.

"The boys make a great frame of bamboo thirty or forty feet long with a great gaping head and long tail. They cover it with red paper and arrange a great lot of lanterns inside; then they fasten long poles to it, light it up, and carry it through the street. They enjoy it immensely, I assure you."

"How about the schools, uncle?" inquired Willie.

"Well, the boys have to commence going to school when they are six years old. By the by, I have a picture of a Chinese schoolmaster here. What do you think of him?"

"I don't think I would like him," candidly replied Henry; and it is safe to say the majority of boys and girls in America would not be attracted to him. But, on the other hand, we must understand that the Chinese are naturally very grave and dignified, and the picture is probably not a true one in that respect. They are also very fond of children. The little fellows are sure to be neat and clean; their big flowing sleeves serve them as pockets, and their boyish nature can not be wholly repressed. However, boys are the only ones considered worth while educating; the girls are left to grow up in ignorance, or a little training at home is considered amply sufficient."

CHINESE SCHOOLMASTER.

"What do they study?" asked Ida.

"Well, the little fellows spend their time in learning to make and pronounce the funny looking characters of their language. The teacher reads a few lines, and the scholars, with primer in hand, follow the pronunciation.

In order to be sure that each scholar is studying, he is expected to study out loud; so you see a school-room is a pretty noisy thing. When a scholar recites, he turns his back on the teacher."

" But what do they learn about?" queried Burt.

"Chinese learning is the driest and most superficial thing in the world. It would take too long to tell you about it. They study the writings of Confucius, who lived some centuries before Christ. It is simply learning good morals; there is no science in it. Whenever you hear about learning

CHINESE SCHOLAR.

in China, it is simply a memorizing of Confucius. But such as it is, it is made the basis of all examination for state purposes. All officers, all mandarins, have to pass an examination. Here, by the way, is a picture of one of these learned Chinese."

" Don't they learn anything about the rest of the world?" asked Willie.

"Of late years the ruling people begin to have clearer ideas of the outside world. But the general impression in China is that the rest of the world is only composed of a few islands off the coast, and that the people all pay homage to China. In a late edition of the Pekin *Gazette* we read about the 'Western nations yielding obedience and returning to a state of peace.' And, to further show you how superstitious the mass of the people must be, I will say that only a year or so ago the most powerful and best informed man in China, Li Hung Chang, the celebrated viceroy, might have been seen

BUDDHIST TEMPLE, CHINA.

prostrate before a little water snake, hoping by this act of homage to put an end to the floods in Northern China."

"What funny beliefs!" exclaimed Ida.

"They seem to us very strange, don't they? But now a word about the religion of China. But first look at this picture of a Chinese temple. In addition to the innumerable superstitious ideas of the Chinese and their worship of the spirits of the dead, they have three systems of religion—Con-

20

fucianism, Taouism, and Buddhism.   I guess I will not take time to explain about these systems, but I hope you will look them up.   Now we must be passing on from China; however big China may be, it is only a small part of Asia.   But, before leaving China, I want to show you a view of Hong Kong. Few know that England has an island in the harbor of Canton, on which is a city under English control.   But that is true of Hong Kong.   You might

HONG KONG.

tell by the looks of the houses that it was not a Chinese town.   However, the majority of the people are Chinese.   The next country that I want to talk about is India.   Now, as you can see on the map, to go from China to India by water we have a long voyage before us, and we have to pass a good many places of interest.   But I think India will furnish us enough to talk about the remainder of the evening.   India, as you know, is a part of the British Empire.   It is as large as all of Europe, not counting Russia; it

THE MAIDAN, CALCUTTA.

contains a population of over 200,000,000; there are more than twenty different languages, and a multitude of religions. So you can see what an interesting section of country this must be. I am going to show you first a view in Calcutta. Point out the city on the map, Burt."

After Burt had found it on the map, and they had noticed its location, Uncle George continued:

"You notice the name of the picture is ' The Maidan.' This is the most beautiful part of the city. It is a great park beautifully laid out in walks and drives; and there, early in the morning and in the cool of the evening, the city people go for the sake of the cool air. I doubt if there is another place in the world where as great a variety of people can be seen. There are representatives of the innumerable people of India and of all the world besides, and all sorts of equipages from palanquins to the finest coaches of European make."

"Ain't there something about a famous ' hole' in Calcutta?" asked Burt, rather doubtfully.

"You are thinking of the 'Black Hole,' I guess. More than 130 years ago, after the English had begun to get a good footing in India, an attempt was made by the Prince of Bengal to drive them out. He took Calcutta, and put 146 prisoners in a room partly underground with almost no ventilation; only twenty-three of them lived till morning. You must read that up in some good history. To change the subject, let Ida read us this account of the scenes along another prominent street in Calcutta."

Taking the book, Ida read the following account about the curious sights to be seen along the Strand in Calcutta: " Every inhabitant of the city, rich or poor, seems to have rigged up some sort of a turn-out and taken his place with his fellows. Some of the groups are very picturesque, and some irresistibly comic. The coachmen in their native costumes, their long beards streaming in the wind; the ladies in their gay dresses, only outshone by the picturesque attire of some native prince dashing along at full speed accompanied by fleet-footed syces. These syces, or Mussulmen grooms, accompany every carriage, and, it is said, will often surpass the horses they accompany in endurance. The natives vie with the Europeans in displaying neat turnouts; some of the native merchants expend fortunes on their stable appointments and equipages."

"That is quite good," said Uncle George as Ida ceased reading. " And

now I will show you a view of this Strand. As I said, it is the name of a
street stretching north from the Maidan. It borders the river bank, and you
notice the shipping in the river. A large majority of the people of India
are Hindoos, and the Hindoos belong to the same great division of the white
race that we do; that is, they are Aryans. Now it is supposed that these
Aryan Hindoos entered India as early as 2,000 years before Christ, but they

ALONG THE STRAND, CALCUTTA.

have become greatly intermixed with the people they found in India; this
accounts for a great many curious things we find in their customs. Nearly
900 years ago, about the time that William the Norman conquered England,
the Mohammedans invaded India, and established themselves in Northern
India. So in the cities of Northern India we find the most interesting ruins
in the country. India, being an English possession, of course there are

338　　　　　　　　　　GATE OF ALA UDEEN, KOOTUB.

railroads. We will suppose we have gone directly from Calcutta to Delhi in the northern part of Hindoostan, the seat of power in the days of Mohammedan rule. The first view I am going to show you is the most beautiful spire or minaret in the world.

It is some eleven miles from the present city of Delhi. It is one of the minarets of a mosque. The mosque was never quite completed. The shaft is nearly 250 feet high; it is built part of the way in red sandstone, and part of the way in marble. You see the shaft tapers regularly to the top. It is divided into five stories, around each of which runs a bold, projecting balcony supported upon large and richly carved brackets, having balustrades that give it a most ornamental effect."

"Is it hollow—can people go up to the top?" asked Henry.

Oh, yes; there is a spiral stairway of 376 steps leading to the top. Once an insane man threw himself from the top and was dashed to pieces at the bottom. Now, here we have another view from

THE KOOTUB.

this same mosque, one of the great arched gateways leading into the mosque. The Kootub mosque is now deserted, but this noble portal still stands. Remember that six centuries have passed, yet the ornaments on that arched gateway, some sixty feet high, still retain their clear, sharp outline. The

next picture is the celebrated Throne Room of their palace. You must understand, however, that all this has been changed since what is known as

THRONE ROOM AT DELHI.

the Sepoy Rebellion in 1857. Let Willie read us this account of this famous hall."

Willie read the following account: "This imperial hall was a gorgeous accessory of the Palace of Delhi. The front opened on a large quadrangle, and the whole stood in what was once a garden, extremely rich and beautiful. The pavilion rested on an elevated terrace, and was formed entirely of white marble. It was 150 feet long and forty in breadth, having a graceful cupola at each angle. The roof was supported on colonnades of marble pillars. The solid and polished marble had been worked into its forms with as much delicacy as though it had been wax, and its whole surface—pillars, arches, and even the pavements—was inlaid with the richest, most profuse, and exquisite designs in foliage and arabesque, the fruits and flowers being represented in sections of gems, such as amethysts, carnelian, blood-stone, garnet, topaz, lapis lazuli, green serpentine, and various colored crystals. A bordering ran round the walls and columns similarly decorated, inlaid with inscriptions in Arabic from the Koran. The whole had the appearance of some rich work from the loom, in which a brilliant pattern is woven on a pure white ground—the tracery of rare and cunning artists."

"And I might add to that," said Uncle George as Willie concluded, "that in that hall once stood the famous peacock throne—a throne most marvelously constructed of gold, silver, and precious stones, and worth an almost fabulous sum."

"What became of it?" asked Burt.

"It was carried off by invading Persians 150 years ago, and was afterwards broken up. But we must not stay longer in Delhi. A little more than 100 miles to the southeast of Delhi is the City of Agra. Akbar the Great, one of the Mongol kings, made it his capital in the sixteenth century, and here are some of the very finest ruins in India. It is scarcely proper to speak of them as ruins, however; they still exist to astonish us with their magnificence."

"Didn't you show us some pictures something like these in some other places?" inquired Nettie. "I am sure you did, but I cannot just remember where," she added.

"I think if you were to recall the Alhambra in Spain, you would notice that it made you think of that. And there is a very good reason for this. Both were built by Mohammedans; both are specimens of Saracenic architecture. Delhi itself is not a very large or important place now, but only a few years ago it was still the capital of the Mongol power in India. I will first call your attention to the mausoleum or tomb of Akbar the Great,

That is said to be the grandest tomb in the world; not the most beautiful, but the grandest. It is 300 feet square, and built in five stories—each story forming a sort of terrace for the one above. The lower stories are built of red sandstone; the topmost one is of marble. You must understand that many acres of ground around this mausoleum are beautifully laid out, and there is a grand entrance and gateway."

MAUSOLEUM OF AKBAR THE GREAT.

"He must have been pretty rich if he could build such a tomb as that," said Henry.

"These Mohammedan conquerors ground every cent out of their subject provinces that they could. The carpets of Akbar's palaces were silk and gold; the hangings on the walls, velvet and pearls; the crown that he wore on his head is estimated as worth about $10,000,000 of our money. One of the customs was once each year to distribute among the people the weight of the Emperor in gold, then in silver, then in perfumes, and so on twelve times."

Henry and the rest of the club were fully satisfied from these statements that Akbar was undoubtedly rich.

MAUSOLEUM OF ET-MAD-OD-DOULAH.

"I have still another view of a mausoleum near Agra. This is the tomb of Chaja Aias, the high treasurer of Akbar. It is generally known by his title, Et-mad-od-doulah. It was built by his daughter, the famous Noor

Jehan, the wife of the celebrated Jehangeer, son and successor of Akbar. By the way, this queen is the 'Nourmahal' of Moore's poem, 'The Light of the Harem." She certainly exerted a wonderful influence over her husband. Let Ida read us a little account of this tomb."

With the beautiful picture before them, the club listened while Ida read the following description. "The building, rising from a broad platform, is of white marble of quadrangular shape, flanked by octagonal towers, which are surmounted by cupolas on a series of open columns. Interiorly and exteriorly this fairy pile is covered as with beautiful lace by lattice work delicately wrought in marble, covered with foliage and flowers and intermingled with scrolls bearing passages from the Koran. Every portion of the mausoleum is thus enriched, and all that wealth could furnish, or Oriental luxury suggest, or genius execute in the completion of the structure, was devoted to its adornment. Each slab of white marble is wrought in rich tracery in the most delicate manner, pierced through and through so as to be the same when seen from either side; the pattern of each slab differs from the next one, and the rich variety, as well as beauty of designs, fixes the attention of the beholder in amazement at the taste and patient skill that could originate and execute this vision of beauty which seems like an imagination rising before the fancy, and then, by some wondrous wand of power, transmuted into a solid form forever—to be touched, and examined, and admired. According to the usage of the Mongols, a lovely garden was planted around the fair shrine, and ample provisions made for its care and preservation in the future. Rare and costly trees, fragrant evergreens, shady walks, and tanks and fountains, all added their charm to set off the central pile."

"Having now shown you these two beautiful tombs," resumed Mr. Adams as Ida concluded, "you will be surprised to hear me say that I am now going to show the most beautiful tomb in the world. It is the celebrated Taj-Mahal. It is about six miles from Agra. It is a mausoleum built for the Empress Moomtaj-i-Mahal, wife of Shah-Jehan. He was the son and successor of Jehangeer, and she was niece of Noor Jehan. Moomtaj-i-Mahal means 'Pride of the Palace;' Taj-Mahal then is simply the last syllable of her name united with the word palace. I will first show you a general view of the grounds themselves. As you might judge from the picture, they are laid out with beautiful taste. The paths are paved with slabs of freestone arranged in all sorts of curious ways. The central avenue leads directly

from the gate to the Taj-Mahal. It is lined with fountains—eighty-four
in number; midway there is a marble reservoir forty feet square, and
this has five fountains—one on each corner and one in the middle. There
are rows of dark Italian cypresses facing the main walk, but there are a
great many trees, or rather groves, fruit trees, the palm, banyan, and graceful
bamboo. There are also great beds of beautiful flowers, so that the air is
loaded with perfume from the banks of roses, from the orange, lemon, and

THE GARDEN GATE, TAJ-MAHAL.

the sweet-scented tamarind tree. Tropical birds are singing in the groves,
and, just outside the wall, the beautiful Jumna River is placidly flowing by.
Such are the approaches to this beautiful tomb. I see that my next view,"
resumed Uncle George after the children had expressed their admiration of
the beautiful grounds, "is that of the gateway opening into them."

"Is that only a gate?" exclaimed Henry.

"That is what it is used for, Henry; but it is one of the most superb
gates in existence. It is large enough and fine enough to be called a palace.

It is built of red sandstone, but inlaid with ornaments, and has texts from the Koran inscribed on white marble."

"What is the Koran, uncle?" asked Henry.

"I should have explained before that the Koran is the sacred book of the Mohammedans. It is their Bible. You notice the arched wall running away to one side? It surrounds the entire garden. Now, finally, I am going to show you the tomb itself, but no picture can do justice to the tomb. It is almost impossible to describe it, but I will make the attempt. The mausoleum itself, the terrace on which it stands, and the minarets are all formed of the finest white marble inlaid with precious stones; the dome is seventy feet in diameter; the height of the Taj, from the terrace to the tip of the golden spire, is 275 feet. It is asserted that the whole of the Koran is inlaid upon the building, the letters being beautifully formed in black marble on the outside, and in precious stones within. Entering the building, in the rotunda you see the beautiful sarcophagi of the Empress and Emperor, his being much the plainer of the two. But the bodies themselves are in two other sarcophagi in the vaults below. You must try and imagine the scene. Above is the lofty dome far up in the distance; the floor is of polished marble and jasper, ornamented with a wainscotting of sculptured marble tablets inlaid with flowers formed of precious stones; around are windows or screens of marble filigree richly wrought in various patterns, which admit a faint and delicate illumination; in the center are the tombs surrounded by a magnificent octagonal screen, about six feet high, with doors on the sides; the open tracery in this white marble screen is wrought into beautiful flowers, such as lilies, irises, and others, and the borders of the screen are inlaid with precious stones representing flowers, executed with such wonderful perfection that the forms seem to wave as in nature, and the shades of the stems, leaves, and flowers appear as real almost as the beauties they represent. Then the tomb of the Moomtaj is singularly beautified; the snow white marble is inlaid with flowers so delicately formed that they look like embrodiery on white satin, so exquisitely is the mosaic executed in carnelian, bloodstone, agate, jasper, turquois, lapis lazuli, and other precious stones. Some of these flowers are formed of no less than eighty different stones, polished uniform with the marble into which they are so delicately inserted that you can hardly trace their joinings. Thirty-five different specimens of carnelian are employed in forming a single leaf of a carnation; and in one flower not

THE TAJ MAHAL, INDIA.

319

larger than a silver dollar, twenty-three different stones can be counted. Yet what I have described can only give you an idea of the beauties spread in profusion over this entire chamber."

There was a moment's silence as Uncle George concluded. The club hardly knew what to say—mere expressions of admiration seemed out of place. Finally Henry ventured the assertion that "it must have cost a lot of money."

"Yes, indeed," said Uncle George; "it has been estimated that at the present day $50,000,000 would hardly replace it. But we must leave Agra with its splendid tombs. The Mohammedan conquerors of India have in their turn been overthrown; but, after all, the vast masses of India have changed but little. At the present day advance is beginning to slowly take place."

"I have read considerable about the strange religious beliefs in India," said Burt.

"I am glad to hear that," replied Uncle George, "it is an interesting field. But I will not attempt to say anything about that to-night. I might say that India was the birthplace of Buddhism. Probably more people profess Buddhism than any other religion. But Christianity will soon overtake it, if it has not done so already."

"Do they believe that Buddha was a god?" asked Henry.

"No, Buddha made no claims to be divine; but the time is far too short to explain about this religion. Buddhism has mainly disappeared from India now, and the old religion of the land, Brahmanism, has regained control. Now there is a great deal that we might talk about in India, but you see it is getting late, and perhaps we had better not go further. And, children," continued Uncle George, "our next meeting will be the last for the present. An old traveler, you know, does not like to settle down. I am going to spend the balance of this year in traveling in the West and in South America. I thought we could not better employ our last evening than to talk about Palestine. To the Christian believer there is no more interesting country. I look forward with a great deal of interest to that evening."

"And say, uncle," said Henry, "is Burt going with you, for sure?"

"I believe that is the talk, Henry," said his uncle with a laugh, "but you must ask Burt."

CHAPTER IX.

THE HOLY LAND.

TIME once more came for the gathering of the club, and this meeting was to be the last for the year. Uncle George was not going away for some weeks, but then it was getting late in the spring, the evenings were growing short, and so, as already announced, Uncle George had decided to make this the last meeting. Probably influenced by this fact, he had made considerable preparation to entertain the club with a little account of Bible lands and scenes. So when the children once more gathered at grandpa's, they found everything ready for them. Uncle George's smile was just as bright as on the first night, and Aunt Mary's welcome was just as warm. We are not sure but the members of the club, by way of atoning for past neglect, looked up with more care some of the points of interest in Palestine. Be that as it may, the children gathered with quite a satisfied feeling around the library table ready for Uncle George to begin his evening's talk; and, as Uncle George was waiting for them, the trip soon commenced.

"Travelers in the Holy Land," began Uncle George, "nearly always take a preliminary trip in Egypt, because it is quite convenient to go through Egypt on our way to Palestine; and then, besides, you know Egypt is quite intimately connected with Palestine, and has a good deal to do with Bible history. Still we will not stop there long. We read in the Bible how Joseph rose to be governor in Egypt. That meant a great deal of power, for the rulers of Egypt did about as they wanted to. It is generally supposed that the mass of ordinary people were little better than slaves. I have here a cut which illustrates that. You see the people are driven to their work with whips."

"What is that thing they are drawing?" inquired Henry.

"Some immense sculptured stone. Now, of course, you are not to

ERECTION OF PUBLIC BUILDINGS.

understand that Joseph ever superintended such work as that, but it will give you an idea of the power of Egyptian rulers. The Bible does not say very much about Egypt. The children of Israel are supposed to have been confined in the Delta of the Nile. Perhaps that is the reason why the pyramids are not mentioned; they were certainly in existence at that time."

"Don't we see the pyramids in that picture?" inquired Ida.

"Yes; only there was quite a large number of pyramids along the Nile, so the ones shown in this cut may not be the ones we mean when we talk about the pyramids. I have here a view of the pyramids near Cairo. Now,

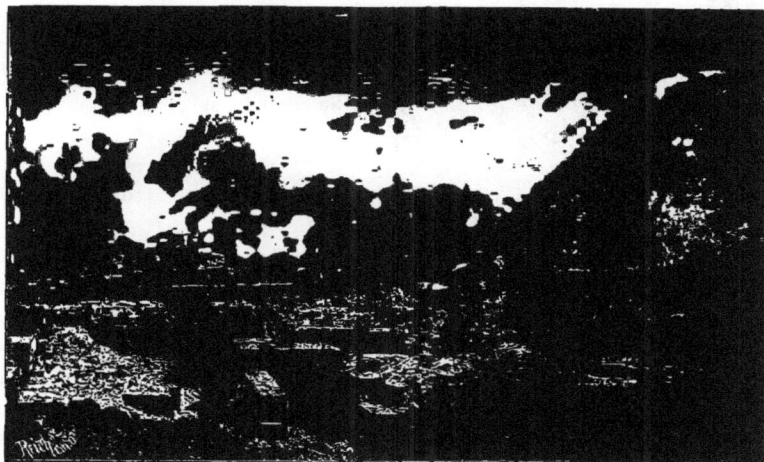

VIEW OF THE GREAT PYRAMID AND VICINITY.

as I remarked, Moses must often have gazed on these pyramids, and it is really strange that he does not mention them. But, of course, the Bible was not intended to satisfy our curiosity on these points."

"Uncle, what do you think they built the pyramids for?" asked Burt.

"There have been all sorts of theories on that point, but of late years we have come very generally to the idea that they are simply the tombs of the various Pharaohs of Egypt."

"Pharaoh is mentioned in the Bible, ain't he?" said Henry with quite a satisfied air.

"The word Pharaoh, Henry, was simply their word for the ruler of Egypt; like president, king, or emperor. The Bible speaks of several different Pharaohs. The one that was probably ruling when the children of Israel were so cruelly oppressed is thought to be the one known in history as Rameses II. And, by the way, that makes me think of a most interesting discovery made but a few years ago; the veritable body of this king was found, and I have somewhere a photograph of the present appearance of the upper part of the body. Yes, here it is. How interesting it is to be able to look at the identical features of this celebrated Pharaoh who lived more than 3,000 years ago, and especially when we think that he was probably the one who severely oppressed the children of Israel."

"Why, I thought that he was drowned in the Red Sea," said Nettie.

"It is generally supposed that the Exodus took place in the reign of his son Menephthah, but you must bear in mind that the Bible does not say that Pharaoh himself was drowned. In fact, the tomb of Menephthah has been found, but not his body. Though the Israelites were in Egypt a long while, the religious ideas of the Egyptians made but little impression on them.

MUMMY OF RAMESES II.

The worship of the golden calf is supposed to be largely owing to Egyptian influence, however. I might say that the Egyptians were noted for the enormous temples they built. The most imposing ruins in Egypt to-day are those of their temples. Here, for instance, is a view of the ruins of the Temple of Karnak. That was at ancient Thebes in Upper Egypt."

"Those big stones," said Henry, pointing to the pillars, "are all covered with pictures, ain't they?"

"Yes; and those strange looking pictures are called hieroglyphics, and

THE HALLS IN THE TEMPLE OF KARNAK.   357

our scholars have learned to read them, and by their means we now know considerable about ancient Egyptian history. They don't look much like our alphabet, do they? But we must not stay long in Egypt, for we must hurry on to Palestine. You remember from the Bible that after the Israelites

CONVENT OF MT. SINAI.

had crossed the Red Sea, the next important stopping point was Mt. Sinai, well down in the Arabian Peninsula. Of course, Mt. Sinai, as being the place where the Law was given, has always been regarded with a great deal of reverence. The Greek Church built a convent there in the sixth century, and I have a view of it shown here. That, of course, is an interesting spot, but then they draw on our credulity considerable by insisting that the convent stands just where Moses saw the burning bush, and there is a magnificently fitted up chapel asserted to be on the spot where the bush stood."

"Didn't you tell us something about the Greek Church when we were talking about Russia?" asked Nettie.

"Yes; you remember I pointed out the difference between the Greek Church and the Catholic Church proper. One of the most interesting items I know of concerning that lonely convent," continued Uncle George, "is that the celebrated traveler, Tischendorf, found there one of the very oldest copies

HEBRON.

of the New Testament in existence. It is a manuscript copy written in the third century; there are only two manuscripts as old as this."

"You say he found it there; didn't they know it was there before?" asked Burt.

"No; the monks were utterly ignorant of its existence. Probably some centuries had passed since they had examined it. But now we will go on to Palestine proper. You see that lies quite a good ways to the north and a little to the east of Mt. Sinai. Now, probably one of the most interesting localities in all southern Palestine is Hebron. I have, as you see, a view of Hebron, and especially the mosque situated in the town. This, of course, is a modern view and trustworthy. When you look at that picture, you must reflect that here was the home of Abraham; the majority of the incidents of his life, as recorded in Genesis, are centered around that place. The cave of Machpelah, where he himself was laid to rest, and where Isaac and Rebecca, and Jacob and Leah were also buried, is supposed by many to be under the dome of that mosque."

"Is that true?" asked Burt. "I mean is that really the place—are there any bodies there?" he added.

JERUSALEM IN THE TIME OF CHRIST.

"Well, as for that," replied Uncle George, "I can only say that the place appears to be very satisfactorily identified with ancient Hebron; that it has always been regarded as a sacred place, and has always been carefully guarded. But it has never been explored by competent parties, and, if it were, probably no bodies would be found. Leaving Hebron, we may as well go directly to Jerusalem. I have a view of Jerusalem which I want you to examine. That is supposed to represent the city at the time of Christ."

"That is a nice looking building?" said Henry, pointing to the temple.

"Yes; that is the temple. Not Solomon's Temple, for that has been destroyed long before. Now, of course, in talking about Jerusalem, there are many interesting things to mention. This was the City of David; this was the city that Solomon adorned; it was here that many of the prophets and heroes of the Old Testament lived and wrote; this was the city that had to withstand sieges from Egyptians, Assyrians, and Chaldeans. And, finally, this was that city that our Lord and Saviour, Jesus of Nazareth, loved—in which he performed many notable deeds, and which was the scene of his cruel death. If we were to visit Jerusalem to-day, we would undoubtedly be very much disappointed in the appearance of the city. It is not an imposing city.

SOLOMON'S TEMPLE.

Its streets are narrow, crooked, and dirty. It reached its zenith of grandeur and power under the reign of Solomon. He it was, as you know, who built the magnificent temple described in the Bible. A great many attempts have been made to picture forth the glories of this temple, but this cannot be done. I have a picture of it here which may help us a little. But if we do not know much about the temple, we do know where it stood—the place that Henry pointed out in the view of Jerusalem. Ida may read this account of this spot." Saying which, Uncle George handed Ida a book with a marked passage.

Ida read the following account: "This area is the most interesting spot in the whole world, sacred alike to Jew, to Moslem, and to Christian;

CHRIST DISPUTING IN THE TEMPLE.

for here it was that Omar had his threshing floor; that Abraham offered up
his son Isaac; that David prayed for the plague-stricken people. Here it
was that Solomon reared that 'holy and beautiful house,' the Temple of the
Lord, wherein were the holy of holies, the ark, the mercy-seat, and all the
poetical symbols of the worship of Israel; here Zerubbabel reared the sacred
temple after that of Solomon had been destroyed; and here was erected by
Herod that gorgeous temple into which our Lord so frequently came, where
His gracious words were spoken and many of His wondrous deeds wrought.
To this spot Mohammed came; and here was built the so-called Mosque of
Omar."

At this point Uncle George called their attention to the view he had of
this famous mosque,
and then Ida finished
reading the account.

"This is the spot
where the one God
was worshipped while
all other lands were
steeped in idolatry;
here were observed
the stately rites and
ceremonies of the
Law; here shone forth
the Shekinah; hither
came up the tribes to

MOSQUE OF OMAR.

the great annual feasts; here came the One who in Himself fulfilled the
types and shadows of the Law and instituted His church. From first to last,
this was the center of the religious, the poetical, and political life of the Jewish
nation. Every Jew regards this spot still as the most sacred upon earth;
every Christian regards it with reverential interest; every Moslem looks
upon it as the most holy place after Mecca."

"But do they know all this to be true?" asked Burt, who seemed to be
somewhat in doubt.

"The temple area itself has never been called in question," replied Uncle
George, though there is a question as to the exact locality of the temple.
But as for the many traditions connected with the spot, we can not decide.

22

It is enough to know that this whole spot was familiar to Jesus; that somewhere in this contracted area stood the temple which he often visited; in which, as a child, he had disputed with the learned doctors. Somewhere in this immediate vicinity he must have stood when he uttered his gracious invitation: 'If any man thirst, let him come unto me and drink.' There is another church at Jerusalem which is of equal interest with this mosque, though it is not as well identified. That is the Church of the Holy Sepulcher. This is a great collection of chapels. It is owned by the Greek, Latin, Copt, and Syrian Churches; that is to say, each of the churches has numerous chapels, and claims jurisdiction over various places of interest; while Mohammedan authorities compel them all to keep the peace. If all that is claimed by these various bodies for the various places shown be true, we have here, collected within a very narrow compass and fully identified, the most interesting places in the world's history. The Greek Church even points out to you the place where the dust was taken to make Adam! It is useless for us to consider whether there is any real support for the identification of these places. This is true, however, that millions of people believe what is here shown, and every year thousands of devout believers worship at these shrines; and we can add further that the events supposed to have taken place at these shrines must have taken place somewhere in the near vicinity, for they are commemorative of the death, burial, and resurrection of our Lord Jesus. You know in the New Testament we have told in simple language how he was crucified, buried, and rose again. Well, entering the church, you are first shown the stone of unction—supposed to be the stone on which the body of Jesus was placed to prepare it for burial. Immense lamps are kept burning over this stone all the time. A few paces further on, in a little railed inclosure, is shown a stone said to mark the exact spot where the mother of our Lord stood while the body was being prepared for burial. Now, I will not undertake to describe all the places shown in this church. They show you, for instance, where the cross is said to have stood; they point out the cleft in the rocks caused by the earthquake, etc. In the rotunda itself we see the Chapel of the Resurrection, and the spot is pointed out where Jesus is said to have appeared to Mary Magdalen when he said, 'Woman, why weepest thou?' And we are shown where she stood when she, supposing him to be the gardener, said: 'Sir, if thou hast borne him hence, tell me where thou hast laid him, and I will take him away.'

CHRIST APPEARING TO MARY MAGDALENE.

"In the rotunda, in which is placed the sepulcher of Christ itself, I have a cut of this room. You see a little marble chapel has been built around the tomb itself. It is a small chapel, twenty-six feet long by eighteen feet wide, and divided into two chambers. The first is called the vestibule or Angel's Chapel; in the center rests a stone set in marble, said to be the one which the angel rolled away from the mouth of the tomb, and on which he afterwards sat. In this little chapel, only sixteen feet long by ten wide, fifteen splendid lamps are kept burning. A low doorway conducts to the

HOLY SEPULCHER.

second chamber, supposed to be the sepulcher itself. This is very small, only six feet by seven, yet forty-three lamps are kept burning. The slab on which the body of our Lord rested, or rather is said to have rested, is much worn by the lips of adoring pilgrims. No one, be his faith what it may, can witness the scenes of passionate excitement, or gaze upon that slab which has been bathed with myriads of tears and kissed by countless lips, without emotion; though there may be grave doubts in his mind whether this be the new sepulcher in which never man was laid, around which Roman soldiers watched after the crucifixion."

The club had been much interested in Uncle George's description of this famous church, and considerable conversation ensued in regard to it.

"We must now," resumed Uncle George, "glance at some of the remaining sights of Jerusalem. I have here a view of the Pool of Hezekiah. In all cities, but especially so in Oriental cities, a supply of water is of the very first importance. Hezekiah was one of the best kings of Judea, and we read in the Bible that he made a pool and conduit, and brought water into the city. It is quite possible that this is the very pool he constructed."

"Is that the same as the Pool of Siloam?" inquired Nettie.

POOL OF HEZEKIAH.

"No; that is a different pool altogether. By the way, a most interesting discovery has been made at the Pool of Siloam within the last few years. A very ancient inscription in the Hebrew language was discovered, which has cleared up quite a number of little points in the Old Testament notices of Jerusalem and its surroundings. It is a pleasure to know," added Uncle George after a moment's pause, " that the more carefully Palestine is investigated and studied scientifically, the more is Old Testament history confirmed.

Our next view is the Jews' Wailing Place. You have all heard of it, and, of course, seen many illustrations of it. This view will give you a good idea of its surroundings."

"What are they all doing there?" spoke up Henry.

"Well, that wall that you see is part of the foundation wall of the temple. They meet here to mourn over the present ruined state of their sanctuary and their nation. No matter what one's belief may be, he can not view the scene unmoved. The place is sacred with the tears of many generations. You may see them any day, but especially on Fridays and

JEWS' WAILING PLACE.

Jewish festival days, putting their heads against the great foundation stones of the temple area, wailing out: 'O God! the heathen are come into thine inheritance; thy Holy Temple have they defiled; they have laid Jerusalem on heaps. How long, Lord, wilt thou be angry—forever?' Pity soon changes to respect before such evident sincerity."

"What do they want?" asked Burt.

"It was, and is, a doctrine among many of the Jews that they are ulti-mately to be restored to power, and that Jerusalem will again be the capital of their land. They hope to hasten this day by their penitence for past wrongs. But let us pass on. Immediately opposite the city is the Mount of Olives. I have a view of it from the city walls. This spot is one of interest; for some Biblical scholars think that the ascension of Christ took place from the summit."

"That looks pretty hilly," exclaimed Henry, "and I don't think it is a very nice place," he added.

But Uncle George said that all Southern Palestine was broken and

MOUNT OF OLIVES.

rugged, and not likely to impress us as a particularly fine country. In this respect the country improves as we go toward the north.

"What are the buildings on the top?" asked Nettie, pointing to the buildings to be seen on the summit.

"That is called the Church of the Ascension. It has no claim to antiquity. Within its chapel is pointed out the rock from which Christ is said to have ascended; but in this instance we need have no hesitation, I think, in deciding that tradition is at fault. Still, we need not feel contempt for the place. Doubtless Christ and his apostles were often in this locality, and somewhere, not very distant, was the scene of the ascension. Leaving Jerusalem for the present, let us look at a view of Bethlehem."

"There was where Christ was born," said Henry.

"Yes; I knew you would all recall that fact. Bethlehem lies to the south and a little to the west of Jerusalem—only about five miles distant.

MODERN BETHLEHEM.

You all know that Palestine is a very hilly, broken country. The town of Bethlehem is situated right on the crest of a hill. The people are noted for their good looks, and they are nearly all Christians. The traveler will find numerous tradesmen who are anxious to sell him some relics. Of course, the great object of interest in Bethlehem is the Church and Cave of the Nativity. That is the place where tradition has it that Christ was born."

"Do they know the exact place, uncle?" asked Burt.

Uncle George could but smile to find Burt so inquisitive on these points.

"About the only reply I can make to that question is, that, candidly, I do not know. Very strong and weighty reasons can be urged against it. But it also remains true that from the very earliest times tradition has connected this cave with the place of his birth. A portion of the church built over this cave is claimed to have been built by the Empress Helena, and to be probably the oldest church in existence. Our main interest centers in the cave under-

CAVE OF THE NATIVITY.

neath the church, where, in a little grotto, is placed a silver star. Countless pilgrims believe that marks the very spot of his birth. You can see in the picture how the cave is adorned by hanging lamps."

"At any rate, Jesus was born somewhere near here, and that may be the very spot," said Nettie.

"Yes, that is true," replied Uncle George. "I might add that near here they show a field claimed to be the very one where shepherds watched their flocks, but I presume no one regards the tradition of any value in this instance. One interesting incident about this town I must not forget to mention. Early in the fourth century, St. Jerome, one of the most illustrious names in the early church, came to Bethlehem to live. Here for more than

DOWN TO JERICHO.

thirty years, beside what he believed to be the very birthplace of Christ, he prayed, and fasted, and studied."

"What did he want to do that for?" inquired Henry.

"Deeply religious minds in all ages have felt like withdrawing from the world for study and reflection," replied Uncle George. "But now let us consider ourselves back to Jerusalem, and let us take a trip down to Jericho."

"That is the place where the walls fell down," said Henry.

"And it is mentioned in the story of the Good Samaritan, too," added Nettie. "But why do they always say 'Down to Jericho,'" she continued.

"It is almost all the way down hill," replied Uncle George to Nettie's last question. "Jerusalem is almost the highest town in Palestine. Jericho, though only a few miles away, is in the valley of the Jordan, some 3,000 feet below. The way leading from Jerusalem past Bethany after leaving Bethany

MODERN BETHANY.

is along a precipitous gorge, and robbers always have infested the place. It is necessary at the present day to be on your guard, or you will still fall among thieves as in the parable. By the way, that tower in the picture is all that is left to show the site of ancient Jericho, though it does not go back to that early time."

"Did you say we went past Bethany?" inquired Burt. "Wasn't that where Martha and Mary and their brother Lazarus lived?"

378 ENTRY OF CHRIST INTO JERUSALEM.

"We can go past Bethany, though the more usual route is through Bethel. I have here a view of Bethany. The modern town of Bethany is a little mountain hamlet known at the present day as El-Lazarieh, deriving its name from the tomb of Lazarus. It must have been a quiet place of retreat at the time of Christ. Just such a place as he would naturally seek to be free from the bustle and confusion of Jerusalem. At the present day Bethany is surrounded by many pleasant gardens, and we know by its ruins that it was once a more important place than now. We may also conclude from the gospel narrative that Martha and Mary must have been in good worldly circumstances. Besides being the place where resided those friends of Jesus whose house was always open for him, it has other attractions for us. Here was the scene of Christ's great miracle, the raising of Lazarus. We are able to trace with all reasonable certainty, for quite a distance at least, the very road from Jericho along which came Jesus with his band of disciples after the death and burial of Lazarus. From the location of the village he could be seen while quite a distance away, and thus the mourning sisters were apprised of his approach and could go forth to meet him. Of course, we can not be sure of the exact location of the grave of Lazarus, but somewhere in this immediate vicinity the great miracle was performed. Here, also, was the house of Simon. We may never know just where it stood, but somewhere near here; and here was the scene of the penitent woman anointing the feet of her Saviour with the precious spikenard; and also near here must have been, I think, the scene of the ascension, for the gospel narrative distinctly asserts that it was near Bethany."

"I thought you said it was Mount of Olives?" said Nettie.

"Some do think so, but I guess the best scholars would decide it was near Bethany. It was from Bethany that Jesus set out on his triumphal entry into Jerusalem. I have often tried to imagine the scene. The morning after the great miracle of the resurrection he sets forth. The road leads up over Mt. Olivet. A great crowd went with him from the village and met a second great crowd coming out of the city. You are all familiar with the story of his entry into the city when they strewed palm branches in his way and cried, 'Hosanna to the son of David! Blessed is he that cometh in the name of the Lord!' It is interesting to know that there is one spot in this road from which the city of Jerusalem bursts into view. Nowhere else on the Mount of Olives is there a view like this; it is peculiarly striking and grand. It is therefore extremely probable that it was at this place that 'He, when He beheld the city, wept over it.'"

The club had been much interested in this account of the scenes and incidents in the life of Christ appropriate to Bethany, but Nettie asked Uncle George some question about Galilee.

"Nearly all travelers," said Uncle George in answer to her question,

MODERN NAZARETH.

"speak in praise of Galilee, and it was probably in its most flourishing state at the birth of Christ. Then it formed quite an important province of the Roman Empire. The first view I am going to show you is that of modern Nazareth."

"Where Joseph and Mary lived?" exclaimed Nettie.

"Yes; where the boyhood days of Christ were passed," added Uncle George. "Here we have no doubt of the location of the place, though we may smile at the simple-hearted villagers when they show us the table at which he ate, the workshop where he labored, etc. Yet the place can not help but possess great interest for all. Near the town there is an eminence from which a magnificent view is obtained. It is surely reasonable to suppose that he often wandered thither and gazed from the rocky summit. To the west the blue line of the Mediterranean is distinctly visible; eastward the plain of Esdraelon spreads its green carpet; behind are the wooded ridges of Carmel, the rocky mountains of Ephraim, and the far off Judean hills; in

JEWISH SYNAGOGUE.

the midst of a circle of grassy hills sleeps the Sea of Galilee. There is one place near Nazareth which seems to be referred to in the New Testament. You know that one time he entered the synagogue there."

"What is a synagogue?" broke in Henry.

"I thought I had explained," replied Uncle George. "Well, here is a picture of one. Services are in progress. A synagogue is a Jewish place of worship. It says that, after his remarks in this synagogue, the people were filled with wrath at him and were about to cast him down a precipice. Well, there is just such a hill right near Nazareth, an almost perpendicular descent of about fifty feet. It is called to this day the Mount of Precipitation."

"Why did they wish to throw him down?" asked Henry.

"Well, Henry, you must read the account in the New Testament. You will also notice how powerless they were against Him, for 'His time had not yet come.' Aside from Nazareth, interest in Galilee centers around the Sea of Galilee, called by several different names. I have here a view of this celebrated piece of water. At the time of Christ the shores of this lake must have presented a very animated scene. Galilee was then enjoying the most

SEA OF GALILEE.

prosperous era in its history. It was a Roman province, and its natural resources were developed as they were never before or since. Galilee was the center of Roman life and luxuriance as far as Palestine was concerned. There were a number of rich and populous cities around the shores of this lake—such as Chorazin, Bethsaida, and Capernaum; and of these, Capernaum, the home of Christ as far as he had any when he came to mature years, was the chief. Let Ida read this extract from the pen of a recent investigator, which will give us an idea of life around the shores of this old lake at the time of Christ."

CHRIST WALKING ON THE WATER.

So, with the club paying close attention, Ida read the following account: "On the shores of this lake might be seen temple after temple rearing their vast colonnades of graceful columns, their courts ornamented with faultlessly carved statues to the deities of a heathen cult. Here were the palaces of the Roman high functionaries, the tastefully decorated villas of rich citizens with semi-tropical gardens irrigated by the copious streams which have their sources in the plain of Genesareth and the neighboring hills. Here were broad avenues and populous thoroughfares thronged with the motley concourse which so much wealth and magnificence had attracted. Rich merchants from Antioch, then the most gorgeous city of the East, and from the Greek Islands; travelers and visitors from Damascus, Palmyra, and the rich cities of the Decapolis; caravans from Egypt and Persia; Jewish rabbis jostling priests of the worship of the sun, and Roman soldiers swaggering across the market places where the peasantry were exposing the products of their fields and gardens for sale, and where fish was displayed by the hardy toilers of the lake, among whom were those whom the Great Teacher selected to be the first recipients of his message and the channels for its communication to after ages."

"I didn't suppose there was anything like that in Galilee when Christ was on the earth!" exclaimed Burt, as Ida ceased reading.

"That is not to be wondered at," replied Uncle George, "for only recent investigators have turned their attention in that direction. Many of Christ's little band of disciples came from the shores of this lake, and all were Galileans. Here many of his mighty miracles were performed. It was on the waters of this lake that the sudden storm arose which was quelled by his voice; and on another time he came walking to his disciples. It was Capernaum where Peter lived, but such have been the ravages of time that we have not yet fully settled just where the town stood. You see the Bible gives us only incidental notices of the places it mentions. It was written to be our guide in spiritual matters only, so but few places have been satisfactorily identified."

"Did Christ and his disciples all live together in one place?" asked Willie. "I thought they moved around from place to place," he added.

"Their headquarters, we might add, were at Capernaum, where Peter had his home; but a short distance away was Bethsaida, where James and John lived. The gathering together of a band of disciples was not peculiar to the work of Christ. It was the custom of the time for any Jewish rabbi, who was a recognized leader, to gather around him a band of disciples, and the relations existing between them was deemed to be very close and of a peculiar nature."

A close observer would have noticed that Uncle George's thoughts were not wholly confined to the subject before him. In fact, the children seemed to have the impression that something was going on not "down on the program," as Willie said afterwards. They knew, in rather a vague way, that

CHRIST AND HIS APOSTLES.

a carriage or so had driven up; they had heard old Watch barking out a good-natured salute; and, in fact, it was already "in the air" that there were visitors in the house. Still, they had been a good deal interested in what they had heard about the Holy Land, and so had not allowed their attention to be greatly distracted. Henry was getting uneasy, and would probably have soon appointed himself a committee of one to investigate the suspicious circumstances. But he was saved this trouble; for, as Uncle George concluded, he held his watch in his hand and apparently cut short his remarks as he noted the time, and rather abruptly closed the albums, though it was plain to be seen that there were still other views to look at.

It was all clear a moment later. For Aunt Mary opened the library door just then, and after an inquiring glance at Uncle George, and observing that the evening's trip was apparently over, invited the club to walk down stairs to the dining room; and when they reached there, they found, to their great delight, the table set for an elegant little lunch. There were actually strawberries and cream, though the former were just a little extravagant at that time of the year. But this was not all, there were also Mr. Charles Adams and wife, the father and mother of Burt and Willie, and Mr. and Mrs. Scott. Though a little surprised, Willie said that the club was still in the ring and ready for business. "But whose idea is all this?" he asked.

"Whose else can it be but Aunt Mary's?" responded Burt. "That is just like her," he added.

Aunt Mary laughed as she replied, "You see I thought my nephews and nieces with their uncle would be ready after their long trip in foreign lands to enjoy a little entertainment at home, and, of course, would want to meet all their friends."

"And," added grandpa, "when celebrated travelers return they generally have a good deal to talk about. Now I think it only fair for each one of you to give us your impressions of foreign travel, and so Willie, as you are the oldest, what part of the trip did you like best?"

Then Willie and the rest talked about their several trips, and told what particular one had interested them most. There was quite a diversity of opinion. Willie decided in favor of Eastern Asia, Nettie of France, Burt of Italy and Greece, and Ida of the Holy Land; but Henry said that one part was as good as the other. And then Uncle George remarked that he believed the club would confirm the judgment of real travelers who, after wandering over the world, quite generally come back with great willingness to America and the United States. "We probably," he continued, "have our share of national prejudice I have spoken about, but Americans of a truth can say that their lines are cast in a pleasant place. I have been thinking that when Burt and I get back next year it might be a good plan to talk about this country and the countries in South America. But, perhaps, that is looking too far ahead."

And so with pleasant talk and laying out bright plans for the future,

the evening passed, and the club adjourned *sine die*, as Uncle George reminded them. And here we bid farewell to the readers, hoping that they
also have enjoyed these little trips, and have learned some items worth re-
membering about "SCENES ABROAD."   •

FINIS.

www.ingramcontent.com/pod-product-compliance
Lightning Source LLC
Chambersburg PA
CBHW030900270326
41929CB00008B/509